THE RELIGION THAT SHAPED AMERICA

An Anthology of Writings Representative of the American Christian Heritage

Dr. Byron Perrine, Editor
Our Christian Heritage Foundation

Our Christian Heritage Foundation

Copyright © 2012 by Our Christian Heritage Foundation. All rights reserved.

ISBN-13: 978-0615689470

Editor's note:

You may think that you know our American Christian Heritage, but do you? America was a VERY religious place at one time. In fact, it WAS the most Christian nation on earth. In the early days of our nation, literally thousands of sermons were printed and circulated throughout the cities and frontier lands of our nation. The "best sellers" of the time were religious books. And, evangelists like Whitefield spoke regularly to large gatherings off Americans eager to hear the word of God.

If you grew up in America in the 1950's, you probably have some frame of reference for the cultural contrast with today. However, what you experienced in the 50's was not the same religious expression that was being experienced in the years prior to the American War Between the States.

One of the main differences between the religion of early America and the religion of the 50's (which many seem to be trying to revive today) was the theological content of the message being preached. Some of you may remember Senator McCarthy (Joseph, not Eugene) of Wisconsin—his name is deservedly associated in our collective memory with the bigotry, fear and division he preached. He was a proper "Christian" in the way of thinking of many, but certainly would not have measured up in comparison to the great religious leaders of early America. Had people then been familiar with the real thing, our American Christian Heritage, they would have recognized the counterfeit when presented with it.

Today we are being presented with a counterfeit. It is being accepted because people are not familiar with the real thing. The vast majority of Americans have never been exposed to the real thing. Our nation as a whole has forgotten its values.

The "real thing" was born of the Enlightenment. Common law was based upon natural law. Everyone understood that the general and special revelations (natural and revealed religion) were complementary in humankind's religious experience, and together provide a proper lens by which to view and understand the world around us. People understood that virtue and happiness go hand and hand, and in the beginning "the pursuit of happiness" meant the pursuit of virtue, this being understood to be the fount of happiness. And, a "Unitarian" preacher could not be distinguished from a "Congregationalist" or an "Anglican" or any other American clergyperson or educated layperson in this respect. We've lost that today, and people don't realize that. They don't even know what they have lost.

The following selections are excerpted from 17th, 18th and 19th Century works, British and American, which have contributed to, and are representative of that American Christian Heritage, now largely and tragically lost from the collective consciousness of the vast majority of Americans.

We are grieved by this loss and pray fervently for revival. It is hoped that these readings will awaken within fellow Americans awareness of how very much has been lost—the richness, the beauty and the truth of the religion that shaped America. All seems daily to be receding further into the mists of a largely forgotten past. "Remember therefore from where you have fallen; repent, return… strengthen the things which remain."

Also included, is a selection from the religious writings of Leo Tolstoy, eccentric to our American experience, yet perhaps of interest, and, a brief selection from Bede. Certainly the universe of Christian writings is far greater than any sampling herein, yet it is hoped this initial sampling will provide a door through which the reader might find entrance into that universe.

These selections have been transcribed into this anthology from the original volumes as cited. **Original spellings** have in many cases been retained, the intent being to preserve the historic flavor of the selections.

—Dr. Byron Perrine, Editor
Our Christian Heritage Foundation
August, 2012

Contents:

The Port-Royalist **James F. Stephen** *p. 1*

The Church **William E. Channing** *p. 5*

Orthodoxy: Its Truth & Errors **James F. Clarke** *p. 8*

Apology for Christian Divinity **R. Barkley** *p. 13*

Our English Bible **H. W. Hoare** *p. 23*

A Christian Directory **Richard Baxter** *p. 30*

Copy of Letter Pope Gregory **Bede** *p. 39*

My Religion **Leo Tolstoy** *p. 42*

Fruits of a Father's Love **William Penn** *p. 49*

Seven Sermons **Robert Russell** *p. 55*

Early Days in the Society **Mary Ann Kelty** *p. 62*

Natural Goodness **T. F. Mercein** *p. 69*

Address **Frederick Beasley** *p. 80*

Satisfaction of Conscience **Charles Rishell** *p. 86*

The Nature of Laws **William Blackstone** *p. 95*

Progress of Liberal Christianity **J. Walker** *p. 102*

American Institutions **Alexis de Tocqueville** *p. 109*

Life of Rev. David Brainerd **J. Edwards** *p. 117*

The English Reader by **Lindley Murray** 124

Sermons by **Joseph Lathrop** *137*

Nature of Religious Truths by **Samuel Clarke** *144*

The Pleasing Companion **J. Torrey, Jun., ed.** *158*

On the Education of Children by **H. Venn** *164*

The Unreasonableness of Indetermination
Jonathan Edwards *168*

The Missionary Work by **W. Slaughter** *176*

Sermons by **George Whitefield**. *179*

Cardiphonia by **Rev. John Newton**. *180*

Practical View of Education **J. Hatchard** *186*

Wonderful Works of God **David Osgood** *192*

Security and Happiness **Richard Price** *196*

Springs of False Judgment **Isaac Watts** *201*

An Earnest Appeal **John Wesley** *205*

Rise and Progress of Religion in the Soul
Philip Doddridge *209*

Extracted from James Fitzjames Stephen, "The Port-Royalists," Edinburgh Review 73, 148 (July 1841): 346

As quoted in William Ellery Channing, "The Church," Philadelphia: J. Crissy, printer, 1841

"But for every labour under the sun, says the Wise Man, there is a time. There is a time for bearing testimony against the errors of (others), why not also a time for testifying to the sublime virtues with which those errors have been so often associated? Are we for ever to admit and never to practice the duties of kindness and mutual forbearance? Does Christianity consist in a vivid perception of the faults, and an obtuse blindness to the merits of those who differ from us? Is charity a virtue only when we ourselves are the objects of it? Is there not a church as pure and more catholic than that of Oxford or Rome--a church comprehending within its limits every human being who, according to the measure of the knowledge placed within his reach, strives habitually to be conformed to the will of the common Father of us all? To indulge hope beyond the pale of some narrow communion, has, by each Christian society in its turn, been denounced as a daring presumption. Yet hope has come to all, and with her, faith and charity, her inseparable companions. Amidst the shock of contending creeds, and the uproar of anathemas, they who have ears to hear, and hearts to understand, have listened to gentler and more kindly sounds. Good men may debate as polemics, but they will feel as Christians. On the universal mind of Christendom is indelibly engraven one image, towards which the eyes of all are more or less earnestly directed. Whoever has himself caught any resemblance, however faint and imperfect, to that divine and benignant Original, has in his measure learned to recognize a brother wherever he can discern the same resemblance.

"There is an essential unity in that kingdom which is not of this world. But within the provinces of that mighty state there is room for endless varieties of administration, and for local laws and customs widely differing from each other. The unity consists in the one object of worship--the one object of affiance--the one source of virtue--the one cementing principle of mutual love, which pervades and animates the whole. The diversities are, and must be, as numerous and intractable as are the essential distinctions which nature, habit, and circumstances have created amongst men. Uniformity of creeds, of discipline, of ritual, and of ceremonies, in such a world as ours!--a world where no two men are not as distinguishable in their mental as in their physical aspect; where all that meets the eye, and all that arrests the ear, has the stamp of boundless and infinite variety! What are the harmonies of tone, of colour, and of form, but the result of contrasts--of contrasts held in subordination to one pervading principle, which reconciles without confounding the component elements of the music, the painting, or the structure? In the physical works of God, beauty could have no existence without endless diversities. Why assume that in religious society--a work not less surely to be ascribed to the supreme Author of all things--this law is absolutely reversed? Were it possible to subdue the innate tendency of the human mind, which compels men to differ in religious opinions and observances, at least as widely as on all other subjects, what would be the results of such a triumph? Where would then be the free comparison, and the continual enlargement of thought; where the self-distrusts which are the springs of humility, or the mutual dependencies which are the bonds of love? He who made us with this infinite variety in our intellectual and physical constitution, must have foreseen, and foreseeing, must have intended, a corresponding dissimilarity in the opinions of his creatures on all questions submitted to their judgment, and proposed for their acceptance. For truth is his law; and if all will profess to think alike, all must live in the habitual violation of it.

"Zeal for uniformity attest the latent distrusts, not the firm convictions of the zealot. In proportion to the strength of our self-reliance, is our indifference to the multiplication of suffrages in favour of our own judgment. Our minds are steeped in imagery; and where the visible form is not, the impalpable spirit escapes the notice of the unreflecting multitude. In common hands, analysis stops at the species of the genus, and cannot rise to the order or the class. To distinguish birds from fishes, beasts from insects, limit's the efforts of the vulgar observer of the face of nature. But Cuvier could trace the sublime unity, the universal type, the fontal Idea existing in the creative intelligence, which connects as one the mammoth and the snail. So, common observers can distinguish from each other the different varieties of religious society, and can rise no higher. Where one assembly worships with harmonies of music, fumes of incense, ancient liturgies, and a gorgeous ceremonial, and another listens to the unaided voice of a single pastor, they can perceive and record the differences; but the hidden ties, which unit them both, escape such observation. All appears as contrast, and all ministers to antipathy and discord. It is our belief that these things may be rightly viewed in a different aspect, and yet with the most severe conformity to the divine will, whether as intimated by natural religion, or as revealed in holy scripture. We believe, that in the judgment of an enlightened charity, many Christian societies, who are accustomed to denounce each other's errors, will at length come to be regarded as members in common of the one great and comprehensive church, in which diversities of forms are harmonized by an all-pervading unity of spirit."

The Following Selection is extracted from "The Church" by William E. Channing Philadelphia: J. Crissy, Printer, 1841, pp. 24 - 34

Editor's note: Grandson of William Ellery, a signer of the United States Declaration of Independence, Dr. William Ellery Channing, 1780-1842, was the foremost Unitarian preacher in the United States in the early nineteenth century.

There is a grander church than all particular ones, however extensive; the Church Catholic or Universal, spread over all lands, and one with the church in heaven. That all Christ's followers form one body, one fold, is taught in various passages in the New Testament. You remember the earnestness of his last prayer, 'that they might all be One, as he and his Father are one.' Into this church, all who partake the spirit of Christ are admitted. It asks not, Who has baptized us? Whose passport we carry? What badge we wear? If 'baptized by the Holy Ghost,' its wide gates are opened to us. Within this church are joined those, whom different names have severed or still sever. We hear nothing of Greek, Roman, English churches, but of Christ's church only. My friends, this is not an imaginary union. The scriptures, in speaking of it, do not talk rhetorically, but utter the soberest truth. All sincere partakers of Christian virtue are essentially one. In the spirit which pervades them, dwells a uniting power found in no other tie. Though separated by oceans, they have sympathies strong and indissoluble. Accordingly, the clear strong utterance of one gifted, inspired Christian flies through the earth. It touches kindred chords in another hemisphere. The word of such a man as Fenelon, for instance, finds its way into the souls of scattered millions. Are not he and they of one church? I thrill with joy at the name of holy men who lived ages ago. Ages do not divide us. I venerate them more for their antiquity. Are we not one body? Is not this union something real! It is not men's coming together into one building which makes a church....

Do not tell me that I surrender myself to a fiction of imagination, when I say, that distant Christians and myself, form one body, one church, just as far as a common love and piety possess our hearts. Nothing is more real than this spiritual union. There *is* one grand all-comprehending church; and if I am a Christian I belong to it, and no man can shut me out of it.... Who shall sunder me from such men as Fenelon, and Pascal, and Borromeo, from Archbishop Leighton, Jeremy Taylor, and John Howard? Who can rupture the spiritual bond between these men and myself? Do I not hold them dear? Does not their spirit, flowing out through their writings and lives, penetrate my soul? Are they not a portion of my being? Am I not a different man from what I should have been, had not these and other like spirits acted on mine? ....

What I wish is, that we should learn to regard

ourselves as members of a vast spiritual community, as joint heirs and fellow worshippers with the goodly company of Christian heroes who have gone before us, in of immuring ourselves in particular churches. Our nature delights in this consciousness of vast connection. This tendency manifests itself in the patriotic sentiment, and in the passionate clinging of men to a great religious denomination. Its true and noblest gratification is found in the deep feeling of a vital everlasting connection with the universal church, with the innumerable multitude of the holy on earth and in heaven….

    I belong to the Universal Church; nothing shall separate me from it. In saying this, however, I am no enemy to particular churches. In the present age of the world it is perhaps best, that those, who agree in theological opinions, should worship together…. Nor do I condemn the union of ourselves to these or any other churches whose doctrines we approve, provided that we do it, without severing ourselves in the least from the universal church…. We must look with undiminished joy on goodness, though it shine forth from the most adverse sect. Christ's spirit must be equally dear and honored, no matter where manifested. To confine God's love or his good spirit to any party, sect, or name, is to sin against the fundamental law of the kingdom of God; to break that living bond with Christ's universal church, which is one of our chief helps to perfection.

Excerpted from Orthodoxy: Its Truth and Errors
by James Freeman Clarke. Boston: John Wilson and Son, 1866, pp. preface-38

Editor's Note: James Freeman Clarke, 1810-1888, was a graduate of Harvard Divinity School, an ordained Unitarian clergyperson, editor of the Western Messenger magazine, advocate of the abolition of slavery, and a member of the "Transcendental Club". He is credited with having suggested to Julia Ward Howe that she write new lyrics to "John Brown's Body"; the result was "The Battle Hymn of the Republic."

….The Protestant Reformation has its Principle and its Method. Its Principle is Salvation by Faith, not by Sacraments. Its Method is Private Judgment, not Church Authority. But private judgment generates authority; authority, first legitimate, that of knowledge, grows into the illegitimate authority of prescription, calling itself Orthodoxy. Then Private Judgment comes forth again to criticize and reform. It thus becomes the duty of each individual to judge the Church; and out of innumerable individual judgments the insight of the Church is kept living and progressive. We contribute one such private judgment; not, we trust, in conceit, but in the hope of provoking other minds to further examinations….

In all great controversies, in the conflicts of ages, where the good and wise have stood opposed to each other, century after century, it is probably that there are truth and error on both sides.

Each side may hold some truth which the other has not seen. There is, therefore, also substantial error on both sides; for each may have failed to see some phase of truth which the other has recognized. But there may be formal error, or error of statement, even where there is substantial truth; for the truth may be overstated, or understated, or misstated, and a false expression given to a true observation.

What, then, is the duty of those who stand opposed to each other in these controversies—of Catholics and Protestants, Christians and Deists, Orthodox and Unitarians? They have plainly a two-fold duty to themselves as well as to their opponents. They ought to increase their insight, and to improve their statements; to deepen and widen their hold of the substance; to correct and improve their expression of the form. The first is the work of religion; the second, that of theology.

The first is infinitely the most important, because the life of the soul depends on the sight of truth. This is its food, without which it will starve and die. But it is also important that it should improve its theology, because a correct theology is a help to insight, and a ground of mental communion....

The fallacy in (Orthodoxy) lies here—that faith is confounded with belief; knowledge with opinion; the sight of truth with its intellectual statement in the form of doctrine. Undoubtedly there is only one faith, but there may be many ways of stating it in the form of opinion. Moreover, no man, no church, no age, sees the whole of truth. Truth is multi-lateral, but men's

minds are unilateral. They are mirrors which reflect, and that
imperfectly, the side of the object which is towards them. Therefore even knowledge in any finite mind is partial, consequently imperfect, and consequently needs other knowledge to complete it.

    This, apparently, is what the apostle Paul means (I Cor. 18:8-12) in his statement concerning the relation between knowledge and love. Knowledge (Gnosis) "shall pass away." The word here used is elsewhere translated by "destroyed," "brought to naught," "abolished," "made of none effect." "Knowledge" here probably refers to definite and systematic statements of real insights. It is something more than opinion, but something less than faith. Faith abides, but knowledge passes away. Faith abides, because it is a positive sight of truth. It is an experience of the soul, by which it opens itself in trust, and becomes receptive of spiritual influence. Faith, therefore, remains, and its results are permanent in the soul. They make the substance of our knowledge as regards the spiritual world. This substance becomes a part of the soul itself, and constitutes a basis of self-consciousness as real as is its experience of the external world....

    All the sects of Christendom do, indeed, place faith at the root of the Christian life; but some make it essentially an intellectual act, others essentially affectionate, and others an act of will. Orthodoxy makes it, in substance, a sight of faith, or an act of looking at spiritual realities. Sometimes it is called a realizing sense of spiritual things. But, at all events, the sight of truth is considered the beginning and root of religion by the Orthodox party in the Church. We are saved by the word of truth; and the Saviour himself is called "the Word,"—belief in whom constitutes eternal life. Rationally, it is argued that the essential difference between the Christian and the unbeliever, or the unchristian, must lie in seeing Christ or not seeing him. The first step in the religious life always consists in looking at the truth….

Religion originates at every moment, from looking at truth. Now, there are four kinds of looking; *faith* which is intuitive looking; *knowledge*, which is the intuition itself looked at by reflection, and so brought to consciousness; third, *belief*, which arranges the products of knowledge in systematic form, and makes them congruous with each other; and lastly comes *opinion*, which does not deal at all with things, but only with thoughts about things. By faith we see God; by knowledge we become conscious that we see God; by belief we arrange in order what we see; and by opinion we feel and grope among our thoughts, seeking what we may find of his works and ways. Every act of faith brings us into the presence of God himself, and makes us partakers of the divine nature. Thus faith is strictly and literally the substance of things hoped for, or the substance of hope. Substance here has its etymological sense, and is the same word in Greek and English, meaning basis, foundation, support, or substruction. It is the inward experience by which we come in contact with invisible things, as

~ 12 ~

perception is the experience by which we come in contact with visible things.

Extract from An Apology for the True Christian Divinity
By Robert Barclay, 1678

(Note: Robert Barclay, 1648-1690, an eminent Scottish Quaker, uses the term "revelation" throughout, which this editor is unwilling to do preferring the term "illumination" for fundamental theological reasons. Barclay maintains that divine inward "revelations" are NOT to be subject to the test of either the outward testimony of the scriptures, or of the natural reason of man which is, in this editor's opinion, quite contrary to the teachings of the New Testament (Mt. 7:15-20; I Thessalonians 5:21; I John 4:1; I Corinthians 14:29). It is the position of this editor that Illumination from the Holy Spirit should never be divorced from but rather complementary to both the General and the Special Revelations, neither of which are private in nature. Notwithstanding, this extract is included in my anthology of treasures of our Christian heritage because of its helpful explanations of the Epistemology of the Holy Spirit, and because of its scholarly references providing convincing evidence that such an epistemology has from the earliest days of the church been foundational and a treasured part of our Christian heritage.)

Inward ("illumination"--see note above) is that which is evident and clear of itself, forcing, by its own evidence and clearness, the well-disposed understanding to assent, irresistibly moving the same thereunto, even as the common principles of natural truths do move and incline the mind to a natural assent….

It is very probably, that many carnal and natural Christians will oppose this proposition; who, being wholly unacquainted with the moving and actings of God's Spirit upon their hearts, judge the same nothing necessary; and some are apt to flout at it as ridiculous; yea, to that height are the generality of Christians apostatized and degenerated, that though there be not any thing more plainly asserted, more seriously recommended, or more certainly attested, in all the writings of the holy scriptures, yet nothing is less minded and more rejected by all sorts of Christians.... Whereas of old none were ever judge Christians, but such as had the Spirit of Christ (Romans 8:9). But now many do boldly call themselves Christians, who make no difficulty of confessing they are without it, and laugh at such as say they have it. Of old they were accounted the sons of God, who were led by the Spirit of God (ibid. ver. 14). But now many aver themselves sons of God, who know nothing of this leader.... Many, under the name of Christians, experimentally find, that they are not actuated nor led by God's Spirit; yea, many great doctors, divines, teachers, and bishops of Christianity… have wholly shut their ears from hearing, and their eyes from seeing, this inward guide, and so are become strangers unto it; whence they are, by their own experience, brought to this strait, either to confess that they are as yet ignorant of God, and have only the shadow of knowledge and not the true knowledge of him, or that this knowledge is acquired without immediate (experience).

    For the better understanding then of this proposition, we do distinguish between the certain knowledge of God, and the uncertain; between the spiritual knowledge and the literal; the saving heart-knowledge, and the soaring airy head-knowledge. The last, we confess, may be by divers ways obtained; but the first, by no other way than the inward immediate manifestation and (illumination) of God's Spirit, shining in and upon the heart, enlightening and opening the understanding.

Having then proposed to myself, in these propositions, to affirm those things which relate to the true and effectual knowledge which brings life eternal with it, therefore I have truly affirmed that this knowledge is no other ways attained, and that none have any true ground to believe they have attained it, who have it not by this (illumination) of God's Spirit.

The certainty of which truth is such, that it hath been acknowledged by some of the most refined and famous of all sorts of professors of Christianity in all ages; who being truly upright-hearted, and earnest seekers of the Lord… the true seed in them hath been answered by God's love… have at last concluded, with one voice, that there was no true knowledge of God, but that which is revealed inwardly by his own Spirit. Whereof take these following testimonies of the ancients.

"It is the inward master (says Augustine) that teaches, it is Christ that teaches, it is inspiration that teaches: where this inspiration and unction is wanting, it is in vain that words from without are beaten in." -- And thereafter: "For he that created us, and redeemed us, and called us by faith, and dwells in us by his Spirit, unless he speaks unto us inwardly, it is needless for us to cry out." (Aug. ex Tract. Ep. Job 3)

"There is a difference (says Clemens Alexandrinus) between that which any one says of the truth, and that which the truth itself, interpreting itself, says. A conjecture of truth differs from the truth itself; a similitude of a thing differs from the thing itself; it is one thing that is acquired by exercise and discipline; and another thing which, by power and faith." (Clem Alex. 1.1. Strom.) Lastly, the same Clemens says, "Truth is neither hard to be arrived at, nor is it impossible to apprehend it; for it is most near to us, even in our houses, as the most wise Moses hath insinuated."

"How is it (says Tertullian) that since the devil always works, and stirs up the mind to iniquity, that the work of God should either cease, or desist to act? Since for this end the Lord did send the Comforter, that because human weakness could not at once bear all things, knowledge might be by little and little directed, formed, and brought to perfection, by the holy Spirit, that vicar of the Lord. I have many things yet (said he) to speak unto you, but ye cannot as yet bear them; but when that Spirit of truth shall come, he shall lead you into all truth, and shall teach you these things that are to come." (Tertullianus Lib. De veland. Virginibus cap. 1)

Gregory the Great, upon these words (He shall teach you all things) says, "That unless the same Spirit is present in the heart of the hearer, in vain is the discourse of the doctor; let no man then ascribe unto the man that teaches, what he understands from the mouth of him that speaks; for unless he that teaches be within, the tongue of the doctor, that is without, labors in vain." (Greg. Mag. Hom. 30. Upon the Gospel)

Cyrillus Alexandrinus plainly affirms, "That men know that Jesus is the Lord by the holy Ghost, no otherwise, than they who taste honey know that it is sweet, even by its proper quality." (Cyril. Alex. In Theasauro lib. 13. C. 3)

Therefore (says Bernard) we daily exhort you, brethren, that ye walk the ways of the heart, and that your souls be always in your hands, that ye may hear what the Lord says in you." And again, upon these words of the apostle, (Let him that glories, glory in the Lord,) "With which threefold vice (says he) all sorts of religious men are less or more dangerously affected, because they do not so diligently attend, with the ears of the heart, to what the Spirit of truth, which flatters none, inwardly speaks." (Bernard in Psal. 84)

This was the very basis, and main foundation, upon which the primitive reformers built.

Luther, in his book to the nobility of Germany, says, "This is certain, that no man can make himself a teacher of the holy scriptures, but the holy Spirit alone." And upon the Magnificat he says, "No man can rightly know God, or understand the word of God, unless he immediately receive it from the Holy Spirit; neither can any one receive it from the Holy Spirit, except he find it by experience in himself; and in this experience the Holy Ghost teaches, as in his proper school; out of which school nothing is taught but mere talk." (Luther. Tom. 5. P. 76)

    Philip Melancthon, in his annotations upon John Chapter 6: "Those who hear only an outward and bodily voice, hear the creature; but God is a Spirit, and is neither discerned, nor known, nor heard, but by the Spirit; and therefore to hear the voice of God, to see God, is to know and hear the Spirit (Phil. Melancthon) By the Spirit alone God is known and perceived. Which also the more serious to this day do acknowledge, even all such who satisfy themselves not with the superficies of religion, and use it not as a cover or art. Yea, all those who apply themselves effectually to Christianity, and are not satisfied until they have found its effectual work upon their hearts, redeeming them from sin, do feel that no knowledge effectually prevails to the producing of this, but that which proceeds from the warm influence of God's Spirit upon the heart, and from the comfortable shining of his light upon their understanding."

    And therefore to this purpose a modern author, viz. Dr. Smith of Cambridge, in his select discourses, says well; "To seek our divinity merely in books and writings, is to seek the living among the dead; we do but in vain many times seek God in these, where his truth is too often not so much enshrined as entombed. Intra te quoere Deum, Seek God within thine own soul. He is best discerned (as Plotinus phrases it) by an intellectual touch of him. We must see with our eyes, and hear with our ears, and our hands must handle the word of life…. The soul itself has its sense as well as the body. And therefore David, when he would teach us to know what the divine goodness is, calls not for speculation, but sensation: Taste, and see how good the Lord is. That is not the best and truest knowledge of God which is wrought out by the labor and sweat of the brain, but that which is kindled within us, by a heavenly warmth in our hearts." And again: "There is a knowing of the truth as it is in Jesus, as it is in a Christ-like nature; as it is in the sweet, mild humble, and loving Spirit of Jesus, which spreads itself, like a morning sun, upon the souls of good men, full of light and life. It profits little to know Christ himself after the flesh; but he gives his Spirit to good men, that searches the deep things of God." And again: "It is but a thin airy knowledge that is got by mere speculation, which is ushered in by syllogisms and demonstrations; but that which springs forth from true goodness, is (as Origen speaks,) it brings such a divine light into the soul, as is more clear and convincing than any demonstration.

    That this certain and undoubted method of the true knowledge of God hath been brought out of use, hath been none of the least devices of the devil, to secure mankind to his kingdom. For after the light and glory of the Christian religion had prevailed over a good part of the world, and dispelled the thick mists of the heathenish doctrine of the plurality of gods, he that knew there was no probability of deluding the world any longer that way, did then puff man up with false knowledge of the true God; setting him on work to seek God the wrong way, and persuading him to be content with such a knowledge as was of his own acquiring, and not of God's teaching. And this device hath proved the more successful, because accommodated to the natural and corrupt spirit and temper of man, who above all things affects to exalt himself; in which exaltation, as God is greatly dishonored, so therein the devil hath his end; who is not anxious how much God is acknowledged in words, provided himself be but always served; he matters not how great and high speculations the natural man entertains of God, so long as he serves his own lusts and passions, and is obedient to his evil suggestions and temptations. Thus Christianity is become as it were an art, acquired by human science and industry, like any other art or science; and men have not only assumed the name of Christians, but even have procured themselves to be esteemed as masters of Christianity by certain artificial tricks, though altogether strangers to the spirit and life of Jesus. But if we make a right definition of a Christian, according to the scripture, that he is one who hath the Spirit and is led by it, how many Christians, yea, and of these great masters and doctors of Christianity, so accounted, shall we justly divest of that noble title?....

Having then laid down this first principle, I come to the second, viz. That there is no knowledge of the Son but by the Spirit, or, that the revelation of the Son of God is by the Spirit....

That which is spiritual can only be known and discerned by the Spirit of God. But the revelation of Jesus Christ, and the true and saving knowledge of him, can only be known and discerned by the Spirit of

God….

"No man can say that Jesus is Lord, but by the Holy Ghost" (I Co. 12:3). This scripture, which is full of truth, and answers full well to the enlightened understanding of the spiritual and real Christian, may perhaps prove very strange to the carnal and pretended follower of Christ, by whom perhaps it hath not been so diligently remarked. Here the apostle doth so much require the Holy Spirit in the things that relate to a Christian, that he positively avers, we cannot so much as affirm Jesus to be the Lord without it, which insinuates no less, than that the spiritual truths of the gospel are as lies in the mouths of carnal and unspiritual men, for though in themselves they be true, yet are they not true as to them, because not known, nor uttered forth in and by that principle and spirit that ought to direct the mind and actuate it; in such things they are no better than the counterfeit representations of things in a comedy; neither can it be more truly and properly called a real and true knowledge of God and Christ, than the actions of Alexander the Great, and Julius Caesar, if now transacted upon a stage, might be called truly and really their doings, or the persons representing them might be said truly and really to have conquered Asia, overcome Pompey, etc….

(In summary, let us end with…) the promise of Christ in these words , "And I will pray the Father, and he will give you another Comforter, that he may abide with you forever. Even the Spirit of truth, whom the world cannot receive, because it sees him not, neither knows him, but ye know him, for he dwells with you, and shall be in you" (John 14:16-17). Again, verse 26-27, "But the Comforter, which is the Holy Ghost, whom the Father will send in my name, he shall teach you all things, and bring all things to your remembrance. But when the Spirit of truth shall come, he shall lead you into all truth …."

Excerpted from Our English Bible
by H. W. Hoare
London: John Murray, 1911
pp. 28-34

At a time when our rude ancestors were quite unqualified to receive instruction in a written form, portions of the Bible-story began to be sung in their ears in the well-known strains of that old Teutonic minstrelsy which was their delight, and even in the very terms of the familiar Saxon warfare. For, in the poetry of the Caedmonic cycle, the Abraham of Hebrew history will be found figuring in battle as a genuine Saxon Atherling, while the Israelites themselves fight with all the savage fierceness of the hosts of Penda.

Nor was this minstrelsy confined to the monastic circle, but its songs were sung before the King and his warriors, and among the peasantry and artisans of the village and the homestead. Other and later poets, such as Cynewulf, seem to have caught something of Caedmon's primitive inspiration, though they sound a more reflective and self-conscious note than his. Through his means, and through theirs, the Scripture narratives circulated for many generations throughout the North, and the common folk acquired, in a form which fixed itself in their memories, a rudimentary Bible-knowledge to which, otherwise, they must for long have remained strangers….

The wide and enduring popularity of the

religious vernacular poetry shows clearly the natural attraction which, especially in its narratives, the Bible must have had for the Teutonic imagination. Nor is there anything in this to cause surprise. For if on its lower side the Saxon temperament had its elements of fierceness, of coarseness, and of sensuality, it was not wanting in a higher side. Our ancestors brought over with them many a mental feature which developed itself, as time went on, and became more marked under the influence of a higher faith. Among such features we may point to their deep sense of the divine in nature, their grave moral earnestness, their loyalty, their practical turn of mind, their love of poetry and song, their wistful curiosity about the unseen world. All these combined together to form a complex consciousness which responded eagerly to the preaching of the monks, and to the natural influence, upon wild untutored impulses, of the ordered austerity and self-effacement of the early monastic ideal which yet in its untarnished freshness. It was not long indeed before the monasteries began to degenerate into mere cities of refuge, within which men and women sought to escape from a world in which they had become either to effeminate, or too ascetic, or too indolent, to work and fight. But at first these scattered houses were the only local centres of spiritual life and light, the only fortresses which could give shelter to those single-hearted pioneers of Christianity who went forth, as "the chivalry of God," not to escape from, but to battle bravely with the world, and to redeem it as best they might from the bondage of ignorance and of sin.

While Caedmon was singing in the North, the popular poetry was being utilized in the South for the purpose of religious instruction by Aldhelm (Aldhelm made a translation of the Psalter, but whether we now possess it is uncertain), Abbot of Malmesbury. Impressed with the sense of how little the peasantry seemed to care for his English sermons, the good abbot, who was one of the most skillful musicians of his day, took up his position in the garb of a minstrel on a bridge over which they had to pass, and having first enthralled his audience by the sweetness with which he sang, he presently attuned his song to a religious note, and so by the magic spell of the Muses won over to a better life many an uncultured soul whom a homily would have only sent to sleep, and whom even the terrors of excommunication would have left lamentably unmoved.

But it was not to the ear alone that the missionaries made their earliest appeal. The momentous decision of the Whitby Conference, in A.D. 664 had caused Northumbria to break with Iona and Celtic Christianity, and to follow the rule of Canterbury and Rome (Green's History of the English People (1877), vol. I., pp. 56-7). By that decision England lost much, but gained even more than she lost. She lost the fervor of Celtic enthusiasm, and the earnest simplicity of the Celtic missionary spirit. But the Celt was better suited to win converts than to train and manage them when won. Through Rome England gained the power of organization, the power to develop herself into a national Church, while she was preserved from the sterility and narrowness which are born of spiritual isolation. The local centre of gravity was transferred from the monastery to the bishop, the unity which was an indispensable condition of her advancement was made possible, and the infant Church, now become once for all an integral part of the religious system of the West, was placed in permanent touch with what remained of Roman civilization and culture. The change soon made itself felt in many ways, and in none more significantly than in the rich embellishment and beautification of church interiors.

Benedict Biscop, Abbot of Wearmouth towards the close of the seventh century, brought over from Rome a number of religious paintings, which he arranged in his churches so as to present to the wandering and curious eyes of those who were unable to read, the chief scenes in the lives of patriarchs and of apostles, of the Virgin and of Jesus.

(In Bede's *Life of the Abbot of Wearmouth* we read)... "The most illiterate peasant could not enter the church without receiving profitable instruction. He beheld the lovable face of Christ and His Saints, or learned from looking at them the important mysteries of the Incarnation and Redemption, or he was induced by the sight of the Last Judgment to descend into his own breast and to deprecate the anger of the Almighty."

In this manner was the story of the Bible gently yet forcibly brought home to ignorant worshippers from the countryside through the ministry of poetry and art, and a kind of rude preparation made for the miracle-plays, the religious drama, and the Biblia Pauperum of later centuries. But the peasantry were not the only class who in these early days were calling for an interpreter. As converts multiplied, so did the need increase for parish priests to minister among them and to teach them, while to the large majority of such native clergy Latin would naturally be an unknown tongue. Bede speaks of these native clergy as "Sacerdotes idiotae," by which he means priests who knew only Anglo-Saxon, and he tells us that it was mainly for their guidance and use that he often busied himself, and that he encouraged other scholars to busy themselves, in translating into the vernacular the Lord's Prayer and the Creed. As bearing on this point we may quote an injunction to parish priests which appears in the canons of Aelfic, Abbot of Ensham, in the century before the Norman invasion: "The mass-priest shall on Sundays and mass days tell to the people the sense of the Gospel in English, and so too of the Pater Noster and the Creed. Blind is the teacher if he know not booklearning."

It is to be feared, however, that this not very exalted standard was often far above the attainment of the country parson of the tenth century.

Bede also translated into Anglo-Saxon the Gospel of St. John, and perhaps we may infer from his selection of the fourth gospel for his purpose that the tree earlier ones had been translated already. In him, therefore, we have the first link in the chain of translators, which through Wycliffe, Tyndale, Coverdale, and their successors in the continuous work of revision, binds the eighth to the nineteenth century in the history of the English Bible. Cuthbert, one of Bede's devoted followers, has told us the story of the completion of his master's labours, and a very touching story it is (Cuthbert's Letter to Cuthwine). Through the whole of the Eve of Ascension Day, 735 A.D., the grand old monk of Jarrow, the ablest scholar of his time in Europe, had been dictating, though with waning strength, his vernacular version of St. John. Evening came on, and then the night, but there still remained one chapter untranslated. "Most dear master," they reminded him when morning broke, "there is one chapter yet to do." "Take then your pen", he said, "and write quickly." The spirit indeed was willing but the flesh, was fast failing, and one by one the brethren came to his bedside to say their last farewells. Then, as darkness again began to close in, the little scribe whose place it was to be near him bent down and whispered, "Master, even now there is one sentence more," and he answered him, "Write on fast." And the boy wrote on and cried, "See, dear master, it is finished now." "Yes," murmured the dying Saint, "you speak well, it is finished now. Take therefore my head into your hands and lay me down opposite my holy place, where it was my wont to pray." And so, on the pavement of his little cell, they laid him down, and with the "Gloria" on his lips the aged monk delivered up his spirit, and departed hence to the heavenly kingdom.

Nothing has come down to us of Bede's English work. No doubt it perished together with many other treasures of the Northumbrian monasteries when the Danes laid the land waste.

Excerpted from
A Christian Directory: Or, A Summ of Practical Theologie, and Cases of Conscience

Pages 47-49, Directions for Young Christians, #8, "Against Uncharitableness and Schism"
by Richard Baxter
London: Printed by Robert White, 1673

Editor's note: Richard Baxter, 1615-1691, was an English Puritan church leader.

    Keep right apprehensions of the excellency of Charity and Unity among believers, and receive nothing hastily that is against them; especially take heed lest under the pretence of their Authority, their Number, their Soundness, or their Holiness, you too much addict yourselves to any Sect or Party, to the withdrawing of your special Love and just Communion from other Christians, and turning your Zeal to the interest of your Party, with a neglect of the common interest of the Church: But Love a Christian as a Christian, and promote the Unity and welfare of them all.

    Use often to read and well consider the meaning and reason of those many urgent passages in Scripture, which exhort all Christians to Unity and Love. Such as John 11:52 and 17:11, 21, 22, 23; I Cor. 3:10, 17 and 12 throughout; 2 Cor. 13:11; I

Thess. 5:12, 13; Phil. 2:1, 2, 3; I Pet. 3:8; Rom. 16:17; I Cor. 1:10 and 3:3 and 11.18; John 13:35; Rom: 12:9,10 and 13:10; 2 Cor. 13:11; Gal: 5:6, 13, 22; Col. 1:4; I Thess. 4:9; and, I John 3:11, 14, 23 and 4:7, 11, 16, 19, 20, 21.

Surely if the very life of Godliness lay not much in Unity and Love, we should never have had such words spoken of it, as here you find. *Love* is to the soul, as our Natural heat is to the Body: whatever destroyeth it, destroyeth Life, and therefore cannot be for our good. Be certain, that opinion, course or motion tends to *death*, that tends to abate your Love to your Brethren, much more which under pretence of zeal, provoketh you to hate and hurt them. To Divide the Body, is to kill it or to maim it: Dividing the essential necessary parts, is killing it. Cutting off any integral part, is maiming it. The first can never be an act of friendship, which is the most that an enemy can do. The second is never an act of friendship, but when the cutting off a member which may be spared is of absolute necessity to the saving of the whole man, from the worse division between soul and body. By this judge what friends *Dividers* are to the Church, and how well they are accepted of God.

      He that loveth any Christian aright, must needs love all that appear to him as Christians. And when malice will not suffer men to see Christianity in its profession, and credible appearance in another, this is as well contrary to Christian Love, as hating him when you know him to be a true Christian. Censoriousness (not constrained by just evidence) is contrary to Love, as well as hatred is.

There is a Union and Communion with Christians as such: This consisteth in having one God, one Head, one Spirit, one Faith, one Baptismal Covenant, one Rule of holy living, and in loving and praying for all, and doing good to as many as we can. This is a Union and Communion of Mind, which we must hold with the Catholic Church through the world. And there is a Bodily local Union and Communion, which consisteth in our joining in body, as well as mind, with particular Congregations: And this as we cannot hold it with all, nor with any Congregation, but one at once; so we are not bound to hold it with any, that will drive us from it, unless we will commit some sin: Statedly we must hold it, with the Church which regularly we are joined to, and live with: and Occasionally we must hold it with all others, where we have a call and opportunity, who in the substance worship God according to his Word, and force us not to sin in conformity to them. It is not *Schism* to lament the sins of any Church, or of all the Churches in the world. The Catholic Church on earth consists of sinners. It is not Schism to refuse to be partaker in any sin of the purest Church in the world: Obedience to God is not Schism. It is not Schism that you join not Bodily with those Congregations where you dwell not, nor have any particular call to join with them: Nor that you choose the purest and most edifying Society, rather than one that is less pure and profitable to you,… supposing you are at liberty: nor that you hold not Bodily Communion with that

Church, that will not suffer you to do it, without sinning against God: Nor that you join not with the purest Church, when you are called to abide with one less pure.

But it is worse than Schism to separate from the Universal Church: To separate from its Faith is Apostasy to infidelity. To separate from it in some one or few essential Articles, while you pretend to hold to Christ the Head, is Heresy: To separate from it in Spirit, by refusing Holiness, and not loving such as are truly holy, is *damning ungodliness* or wickedness: To differ from it by any error, of judgment or life, against the Law of God, is sin. To magnify *one Church* or Party, and deny all or any of the rest to be Christians, and parts of the Universal Church, is Schism by a dangerous breach of Charity: And this is the principal Schism that I here admonish you to avoid. It is Schism also to condemn unjustly any particular Church as no Church: And it is Schism to withdraw your Bodily Communion from a Church that you were bound to hold that Communion with, upon a false supposition that it is no Church, or is not lawfully to be communicated with. And it is Schism to make Divisions or parties in a Church, though you divide not from that Church. Thus I have (briefly) told you what is Schism.

One pretence for Schism is (Usurped) Authority, which some one Church may claim to Command others that owe them no subjection: Thus Pride which is the Spirit of Hell, having crept into the Church of Christ, and animated Usurpations of

Lordship and Dominion, and contending for superiority, hath caused the most dangerous Schisms in the Church, that ever it was infested with. The Bishop of Rome (advantaged by the Seat and Constitution of that Empire) having claimed the Government of all the Christian world, condemneth all the Churches that will not be his subjects: And so hath made himself the Head of a Sect, and of the most pernicious Schism that ever did rend the Church of Christ: And the Bishop of Constantinople, and too many more, have followed that same Method in a lower degree, exalting themselves above their Brethren, and giving them Laws, and then condemning and persecuting them that obey them not. And when they have imposed upon other Churches, their own usurped Authority and Laws, they have laid the plot to call all men *Schismaticks* and *Sectaries*, that own not their tyrannical Usurpation, and that will not be Schismaticks and Sectaries with them: And the cheat lyeth in this, that they confound the Churches Unity, with their pretended Authority, and Schism with the refusal of Subjection to them. If you will not take them for your Lords, they cry out that you divide from the Church: As if we could hold Communion with no Churches, but those whose Bishops we obey? Communion with other Churches is maintained by Faith and Charity, and Agreement in things necessary, without subjection to them. As we may hold all just Communion with the Churches in Armenia, Arabia, Russia, without subjection to their Bishops, so may we with any other Church besides that of which we are members. Division or Schism is contrary to Unity and Concord, and not to a Usurped Government: Though disobedience to the Pastors which God hath set over us, is a sin, and dividing from them, is a Schism. Both the Pope and all the lower Usurpers, should do well first to show their Commission from God to be our Rulers, before they call it Schism to refuse their Government. If they had not made better advantage of Fire and Sword, than of Scripture and Argument, the world would but have laughed them to scorn, when they had heard them say, *All are Schismaticks that will not be our Subjects: Our Dominion and will shall be necessary to the Unity of the Church.* The Universal Church indeed is one, united under On Head and Governor; but it is only Jesus Christ that is that Head, and not any Usurping Vicar or Vice-Christ. The Bishops of particular Churches are his Officers; but he had Deputed no Vicar to his own Office, as the Universal Head. Above all Sects take heed of this pernicious Sect, who pretend their Usurped Authority for their Schism, and have no way to promote their Sect, but by calling all Sectaries that will not be Sectaries, and Subjects unto them.

Another pretence for Schism is the Numbers of the Party: This is another of the Papists motives: As if it were lawful to Divide the Church of Christ, if they can but get the greater party? They say, *We are the most, and therefore you should yield to us:* (And so do others where by the Sword they force the most to submit to them.) But we answer them, As many as they are, they are too few, to be the *Universal Church.* The Universal Church containing all true professing Christians, is much more than they. The Papists are not a third part (if a fourth) of the whole Church. Papists are a *corrupted Sect of Christians:* I will be against Dividing the Body of Christ into any Sects, rather than to be one of that Sect or divided party, which is the greatest.

Another pretence for Schism, is the soundness or Orthodoxness of a Party: Almost all Sects pretend that they are wiser and of sounder judgment than all the Christian World besides: yea, those that most palpably contradict the Scriptures,
(as the Papists in their half-communion and unintelligible service) and have no better reason why they will so Believe or Do, but because others have so Believed and Done already.

But, 1. The greatest pretenders to Orthodoxness, are not the most Orthodox: 2. And if they were, I can value them for that in which they excel, without abating my due respect to the rest of the Church. 3. For the whole Church is Orthodox in all the Essentials of Christianity; or else they were not Christians: And I must love all that are Christians with that special Love that's due to the members of Christ, though I must superadd such esteem for those that are a little wiser or better than others, as they deserve.

The fourth pretence for Schism, is the Holiness of the party that men adhere to. But this must make but a gradual difference in our esteem and love to some Christians above others: If really they are most Holy, I must Love them most, and labour to be as Holy as they: But I must not therefore unjustly deny communion or due respect to other Christians that are less holy: nor cleave to them as a Sect or divided party whom I esteem most holy. For the holiest are most charitable, and most against the divisions among Christians, and tenderest of their Unity and Peace.

The sum of this Direction is: 1. Highly value Christian Love and Unity: 2. Love those most that are most Holy, and be most familiar with them for your own edification: and if you have your choice, hold local personal communion, with the soundest, purest and best qualified Church. 3. But entertain not hastily any odd opinion of a divided party: or if you do hold it as an opinion, lay not greater weight on it, than there is cause. 4. Own the best as best, but none as a divided Sect; and espouse not their dividing interest. 5. Confine not your special Love to a party, especially for agreeing in some opinions with you: but extend it to all the members of Christ. 6. Deny not local communion, when there is occasion for it, to any Church that hath the substance of true Worship, and forceth you not to sin. 7. Love them as true Christians and Churches, even when they thus drive you from their communion.

It is a most dangerous thing to a young Convert, to be ensnared in a Sect: It will before you are aware, possess you with a feavorish sinful Zeal, for the Opinions and interests of that Sect: It will make you bold in bitter invectives and censures against those that differ from the: It will corrupt your Church-communion, and fill your very prayers with partiality and humane passions: It will secretly bring malice under the name of Zeal, into your minds and words: In a word, it is a secret, but deadly enemy to Christian Love and Peace. Let them that are wiser and more Orthodox and Godly than others, shew it as the Holy Ghost directeth them: James 3:13, 14, 15, 16, 17, 18. *[Who is a wise man, and endued with knowledge among you? Let him shew out of a good conversation, his works with meekness of wisdom. But if ye have bitter envying (or zeal) and strife in your hearts, glory not and lie not against the truth: This wisdom descendeth not from above, but is earthly, sensual, divelish: For where envying and strife is, there is confusion (or tumult) and every evil work: But the wisdom that is from above, is first Pure, then Peaceable, gentle, easie to be intreated, full of mercy and good fruits, without partiality (or wrangling) and without hypocrisie. And the fruit of righteousness is sown in peace of them that make peace.]*

A Copy of the letter which Pope Gregory sent to the Abbot Mellitus, then going into Britain (A.D. 601)

Preserved by the Venerable Bede in his
Ecclesiastical History of England
J. A. Giles edition
London: Henry G. Bohn, 1847, pp. 55-56

"To his most beloved son, the Abbot Mellitus; Gregory; the servant of the servants of God. We have been much concerned, since the departure of our congregation, that is with you, because we have received no account of the success of your journey. When, therefore, Almighty God shall bring you to the most reverend Bishop Augustine, our brother, tell him what I have, upon mature deliberation on the affair of the English, determined upon, viz., that the temples of the idols in that nation ought not to be destroyed; but let the idols that are in them be destroyed; let holy water be made and sprinkled in the said temples, let altars be erected, and relics placed. For if those temples are well built, it is requisite that they be converted from the worship of devils to the service of the true God; that the nation, seeing that their temples are not destroyed, may remove error from their hearts, and knowing and adoring the true God, may the more familiarly resort to the places to which they have been

accustomed. And because they have been used to slaughter many oxen in the sacrifices to devils, some solemnity must be exchanged for them on this account, as that on the day of the dedication, or the nativities of the holy martyrs, whose relics are there deposited, they may build themselves huts of the boughs of trees, about those churches which have been turned to that use from temples, and celebrate the solemnity with religious feasting, and no more offer beasts to the Devil, but kill cattle to the praise of God in their eating, and return thanks to the Giver of all things for their sustenance; to the end that, whilst some gratifications are outwardly permitted them, they may the more easily consent to the inward consolations of the grace of God. For there is no doubt that it is impossible to efface every thing at once from their obdurate minds; because he who endeavours to ascend to the highest place, rises by degrees or steps, and not by leaps. Thus the Lord made himself known to the people of Israel in Egypt; and yet he allowed them the use of the sacrifices which they were wont to offer to the Devil, in his own worship; so as to command them in his sacrifice to kill beasts, to the end that, changing their hearts, they might lay aside one part of the sacrifice, whilst they retained another; that whilst they offered the same beasts which they were wont to offer, they should offer them to God, and not to idols; and thus they would no longer be the same sacrifices. This it behooves your affection to communicate to our aforesaid brother, that he, being there present, may consider how he is to order all things. God preserve you in safety, most beloved son.

"Given the 17th of June, in the nineteenth year of the reign of our lord, the most pious emperor, Mauritius Tiberius, the eighteenth year after the consulship of our said lord. The fourth indiction."

Except from "My Religion"
by Count Leo Tolstoi
Translated from the French by Huntington Smith
New York: Thomas Y. Crowell & Co., 1885
CHAPTER IX (Abridged)

Editor's note: Lev Nikolayevich Tolstoy, 1828-1910, was a Russian novelist and social reformer. His novels War and Peace and Anna Karenina are acknowledged as two of the greatest novels of all time. While not representative of American Christian heritage, nor contributing to the American experience, this excerpt from the writings of Tolstoy is included because there is within it evidence of the Spirit at work in his heart. Tolstoy's religious writings are thus a part of the broader heritage of the living and universal Christian church of which our American Christian experience is but a part. However, to be sure, his writings have hints of "class warfare" that foreshadow the Russian Revolution, and "ascetic" currents running through them that are quite foreign to the American experience.

Let all the world practice the doctrine of Jesus, and the reign of God will come upon earth; if I alone practice it, I shall do what I can to better my own condition and the condition of those about me. There is no salvation aside from the fulfillment of the doctrine of Jesus. But who will give me the strength to practice it, to follow it without ceasing, and never to fail? *"Lord, I believe; help thou mine unbelief."* The disciples called upon Jesus to strengthen their faith. *"When I would do good,"* says the Apostle Paul, *"evil is present with me."* It is hard to work out one's salvation.

A drowning man calls for aid. A rope is thrown to him, and he says: "Strengthen my belief that this rope will save me. I believe that the rope will save me; but help my unbelief." What is the meaning of this? If a man will not seize upon his only means of safety, it is plain that he does not understand his condition.

How can a Christian who professes to believe in the divinity of Jesus and of his doctrine, whatever may be the meaning that he attaches thereto, say that he wishes to believe, and that he cannot believe? God comes upon earth, and says, "Fire, torments, eternal darkness await you; and here is your salvation—fulfill my doctrine." It is not possible that a believing Christian should not believe and profit by the salvation thus offered to him; it is not possible that he should say, "Help my unbelief." If a man says this, he not only does not believe in his perdition, but he must be certain that he shall not perish.

A number of children have fallen from a boat into the water. For an instant their clothes and their feeble struggles keep them on the surface of the stream, and they do not realize their danger. Those in the boat throw out a rope. They warn the children against their peril, and urge them to grasp the rope (the parables of the woman and the piece of silver, the shepherd and the lost sheep, the marriage feast, the prodigal son, all have this meaning), but the children do not believe; they refuse to believe, not in the rope, but that they are in danger of drowning. Children as frivolous as themselves have assured them that they can continue to float gaily along even when the boat is far away. The children do not believe; but when their clothes are saturated, the strength of their little arms exhausted, they will sink and perish. This they do not believe, and so they do not believe in the rope of safety.

    Just as the children in the water will not grasp the rope that is thrown to them, persuaded that they will not perish, so men who believe in the resurrection of the soul, convinced that there Is no danger, do not practice the commandments of Jesus. They do not believe in what is certain, simply because they do believe in what is uncertain. It is for this cause they cry, "Lord, strengthen our faith, lest we perish." But this is impossible. To have the faith that will save them from perishing, they must cease to do what will lead them to perdition, and they must begin to do something for their own safety; they must grasp the rope of safety. Now this is exactly what they do not wish to do; they wish to persuade themselves that they will not perish, although they see their comrades perishing one after another before their very eyes. They wish to persuade themselves of the truth of what does not exist, and so they ask to be strengthened in faith. It is plain that they have not enough faith, and they wish for more.

    When I understood the doctrine of Jesus, I saw that what these men call faith is the faith denounced by the apostle James:--

    "What doth it profit, my brethren, if a man

believe he hath faith, but hath not works? Can that faith save him? If a brother or sister be naked and in lack of daily food, and one of you say unto them, Go in peace, be ye warmed and filled; and yet ye give them not the things needful to the body; what doth it profit? Even so faith, if it have not works, is dead in itself. But some one will say, Thou hast faith, and I have works: Shew me thy faith which is without works, and I, by my works, will show thee my faith. Thou believest there is one God; thou doest well: the demons also believe, and tremble. But wilt thou know, O vain man, that faith without works is dead? Was not Abraham our father justified by works when he offered up Isaac his son upon the altar? Thou seest that faith wrought with his works and by works was faith made perfect…. Ye see that by works a man is justified, and not only by faith. For as the body without the spirit is dead, so faith is dead without works." (James 2:14-26—Tischendorf text.)

James says that the indication of faith is the acts that it inspires, and consequently that a faith which does not result in acts is of words merely, with which one cannot feed the hungry, or justify belief, or obtain salvation. A faith without acts is not faith. It is only a disposition to believe in something, a vain affirmation of belief in something in which one does not really believe. Faith, as the apostle James defines it, is the motive power of actions, and actions are a manifestation of faith.

The Jews said to Jesus: "What signs shewest thou then, that we may see, and believe thee? What dost thou work?" (John 6:30. See also Mark 15:32; Matt. 27:42). Jesus told them that their desire was vain, and that they could not be made to believe what they did not believe. *"If I tell you,"* he said, *"ye will not believe"* (Luke 22:67); *"I told you, and ye believed not. . . . But ye believe not because ye are not of my sheep"* John 10:25, 26).

  The Jews asked exactly what is asked by Christians brought up in the Church; they asked for some outward sign which should make them believe in the doctrine of Jesus. Jesus explained that this was impossible, and he told them why it was impossible. He told them that they could not believe because they were not of his sheep; that is, they did not follow the road he had pointed out. He explained why some believed, and why others did not believe, and he told them what faith really was. He said: *"How can ye believe which receive your doctrine one of another, and seek not the doctrine that cometh only from God?"* (John 5:44).

  To believe, Jesus says, we must seek for the doctrine that comes from God alone.

  "He that speaketh of himself seeketh (to extend) *his own doctrine, but he that seeketh* (to extend) *the doctrine of him that sent him, the same is true, and no untruth is in him."* (John 7:18.)

  The doctrine of life…is the foundation of faith, and actions result spontaneously from faith. But there are two doctrines of life: Jesus denies the one and affirms the other. One of these doctrines, a source of all error, consists of the idea that the personal life is one of the essential and real attributes of man….

    In men who demand of Jesus that he shall work miracles we may recognize a desire to believe in his doctrine; but this desire never can be realized in life, however arduous the efforts to obtain it. In vain they pray, and observe the sacraments, and give in charity, and build churches, and convert others; they cannot follow the example of Jesus because their acts are inspired by a faith based upon an entirely doctrine from that which they confess. They could not sacrifice an only son as Abraham was ready to do, although Abraham had no hesitation whatever as to what he should do, just as Jesus and his disciples were moved to give their lives for others, because such action alone constituted for them the true meaning of life. This incapacity to understand the substance of faith explains the strange moral state of men, who, acknowledging that they ought to live in accordance with the doctrine of Jesus, endeavor to live in opposition to this doctrine….

    When Jesus told his disciples that they must forgive a brother who trespassed against them not only once, but seventy times seven times, the disciples were overwhelmed at the difficulty of observing this injunction, and said, *"Increase our faith,"*… they uttered the language of would-be Christians: "We wish to believe, but cannot; strengthen our faith that we may be saved; make us believe" (as the Jews said to Jesus when they demanded miracles); "either by miracles or promises of recompense, make us to have faith in our salvation."

The disciples said what we all say: "How pleasant it would be if we could live our selfish life, and at the same time believe that it is far better to practice the doctrine of God by living for others." This disposition of mind is common to us all; it is contrary to the meaning of the doctrine of Jesus, and yet we are astonished at our lack of faith. Jesus disposed of this misapprehension by means of a parable illustrating true faith. Faith cannot come of confidence in his words; faith can come only of a consciousness of our condition; faith is based only upon the dictates of reason as to what is best to do in a given situation. He showed that this faith cannot be awakened in others by promises of recompense or threats of punishment, which can only arouse a feeble confidence that will fail at the first trial; but that the faith which removes mountains, the faith that nothing can shatter, is inspired by the consciousness of our inevitable loss if we do not profit by the salvation that is offered.

To have faith, we must not count on any promise of recompense; we must understand that the only way of escape from a ruined life is a life conformable to the will of the Master. He who understands this will not ask to be strengthened in his faith, but will work out his salvation without the need of any exhortation....

Excerpted from
Fruits of a Father's Love: Being the Advice of William Penn to His Children,
Relating to Their Civil and religious Conduct

The Eighth Edition

Philadelphia: Printed by Benjamin Johnson, 1792, pp. 17-19; 77-84.

Editor's note: William Penn, 1644-1718, was a Quaker, the founder of Pennsylvania, and an early champion of democracy and religious freedom.

Having thus expressed my self to you, my dear children, as to the things of God, his truth and kingdom, I refer you to his light, grace, spirit and truth within you, and to the holy scriptures of truth without you, which from my youth I loved to read, and were ever blessed to me; and which I charge you to read daily; the Old Testament for comfort and hope, but especially the New Testament for doctrine, faith and worship: for they were given forth by holy men of God in divers ages, as they were moved of the Holy Spirit; and are the declared and revealed mind and will of the holy God to mankind under divers dispensations, and they are certainly able to make the man of God perfect, through faith, unto salvation; being such a true and clear testimony to the salvation that is of God, through Christ the second Adam, the light of the world, the quickening Spirit, who is full of grace and truth, whose light, grace, spirit and truth, bear witness to them in every sensible soul, as they frequently, plainly and solemnly bear testimony to the light, spirit, grace and truth, both in himself and in and to his people, to their sanctification, justification, redemption and consolation, and in all men to their visitation, reproof and conviction in their evil ways: I say, having thus expressed myself in general, I refer you, my dear children, to the light and spirit of Jesus, that is within you, and to the scriptures of truth without you, and such other testimonies to the one same eternal truth, as heave been borne in our day; and shall now descend to particulars, that you may more directly apply what I have said in general, both as to your religious and civil direction in your pilgrimage upon earth....

    Temperance I most earnestly recommend to you, throughout the whole course of your lives: It is numbered amongst "The fruits of the Spirit," Gal. 5:23, and is a great and requisite virtue. Properly and strictly speaking, it refers to diet; but, in general, may be considered as having relation to all the affections and practices of men. I will therefore begin with it in regard to food, the sense in which it is customarily taken. Eat to live, and not live to eat, for that is below a beast. Avoid curiosities and provocations; let your chiefest sauce be a good stomach, which temperance will help to get you. You can not be too plain in your diet, so you are clean; nor too sparing, so you have enough for nature. For that which keeps the body low, makes the spirit clear, as silence makes it strong.

It conduces to good digestion, that to good rest, and that to a firm constitution. Much less feast any, except the poor; as Christ taught, Luke 14:12-13. For entertainments are rarely without sin; but receive strangers readily. As in diet so in apparel, observe, I charge you, and exemplary plainness. Chuse your clothes for their usefulness, not the fashion, and for covering and not finery, or to please a vain mind in yourselves or others: they are fallen souls, that think clothes can give beauty to man. "The life is more than raiment," Mat. 6:25. Man cannot men God's work, who can give neither life nor parts. They shew little esteem for the wisdom and power of their Creator, that under-rate his workmanship (I was going to say, his image) to a taylor's invention: gross folly and profanity! But do you, my dear children, call to mind who they were of old, that Jesus said, took so much care about what they should eat, drink, and put on: were they not Gentiles, heathens, a people without God in the world? Read Mat. 6 and when you have done that, peruse those excellent passages of the apostles Paul and Peter, I Tim. 2:9-10 and I Pet. 3:3... where, if you find the exhortation to women only, conclude it was effeminate, and a shame then for men to use such arts and cost upon their persons. Follow you the example of those primitive Christians, and not voluptuous Gentiles, that perverted the very order of things: for they set lust above nature, and the means above the end, and preferred vanity to conveniency; a wanton excess, that has no sense of God's mercies, and therefore cannot make a right use of them, and less yield the returns they deserve. In short, these intemperances are great enemies to health and to posterity; for they disease the body, rob children, and disappoint charity, and are of evil example; very catching, as well as pernicious evils. Nor do they end there: they are succeeded by other vices, which made the apostle put them together in his epistle to the Galatians, chap. 5:20-21. The evil fruits of this part of intemperance, are so many and great, that, upon a serious reflection, I believe there is not a country, town, or family, almost, that does not labour under the mischief of it. I recommend to your perusal, the first part of No Cross no Crown, and of the Address to Protestants, in which I am more particular in my censure of it: as are the authorities I bring in favour of moderation. But the virtue of temperance does not only regard eating, drinking, and apparel, but furniture, attendance, expence, gain, parsimony, business, diversion, company, speech, sleeping, watchings, and every passions of the mind, love, anger, pleasure, joy, sorrow, resentment, are all concerned in it: therefore bound your desires, teach your wills subjection, take Christ for your example, as well as guide. It was he that led and taught a life of faith in Providence, and told his disciples the danger of the cares and pleasures of this world; they choaked the seed of the kingdom, stifled and extinguished virtue in the soul, and rendered man barren of good fruit. His Sermon upon the Mount is one continued divine authority in favour of an universal temperance. The apostle, well aware of the necessity of this virtue, gave the Corinthians a seasonable caution. 'Know ye not,' says he, 'that they which run in a race, run all, but one receiveth the prize? So run that ye may obtain. And every man that striveth for mastery, (or seeketh victory) is temperate in all things: (he acts discreetly, and with a right judgment.) Now, they do it to obtain a corruptible crown, but we an incorruptible. I therefore so run not as uncertainly; so fight I, not as one that beateth the air: but I keep under my body, and bring it into subjection; lest that by any means, when I have preached to others, I myself should be a castaway,' I Cor. 9:24-27. In another chapter he presses temperance almost to indifferency: "But this I say, brethren, the time is short: it remained, that both they that have wives, be as though they had none; and they that weep, as though they wept not; and they that rejoice, as though they rejoiced not; and they that use this world, as not abusing it." And all this is not without reason: he gives a very good one for it: "For, (saith he) the fashion of the world passeth away: but I would have you without carefulness," I Cor. 7:29, 32. It was for this cause he pressed it so hard upon Titus to warn the elders of that time to be "Sober, grave, temperate," Tit. 2:2, not eager, violent, obstinate, tenacious, or inordinate in any sort. He makes it an indispensable duty in pastors of churches, that they be "Not self-willed, not soon angry, nor given to wine or filthy lucre, but lovers of hospitality, of good men, sober, just, holy, temperate, Tit. 1:7-8. And why so? Because against these excellent virtues there is no law, Gal. 5:23,ff.

I will shut up this head (being touched upon in divers places of this Advice) with this one most comprehensive passage of the Apostle, "Philip. 4:5. "Let your moderation be known unto all men, the Lord is at hand." As if he had said, Take heed; look to your ways; have a care what you do; for the Lord is near you, even at the door: he sees you, he marks your steps, tells your wanderings, and he will judge you. Let this excellent, this home and close sentence live in your minds: let it ever dwell upon your spirits, my beloved children, and influence all your actions, aye, your affections and thoughts. It is a noble measure, sufficient to regulate the whole; they that have it, are easy as well as safe. No extreme prevails; they world is kept at arm's-end; and such have power over their own spirits, which give them the truest enjoyment of themselves and what they have: a dominion greater than that of empires. O may this virtue be yours! You have grace from God for that end, and it is sufficient: employ it, and you cannot miss of temperance, nor therein of the truest happiness in all your conduct....

Extracted From

Seven Sermons by Robert Russell

Sermon Five: "Joshua's Resolution to Serve the Lord"
London: Printed for Hawes, Clarke and Collins by S. Crowder and E. Johnston, 1778

Editor's note: During the 18th Century thousands of sermons were printed in America. Among them, Robert Russell's "best selling" <u>Seven Sermons</u>. These sermon's, and many like them, played an important role in in the development of American Christianity by providing guidance to the many Americans who were part of congregations not yet having a permanent minister.

Josh. xxiv. Part of Verse 15.
But as for me and my house, we will serve the
L O R D.

….Sin is so sweet unto a wicked man, the world and the flesh is so bewitching, that notwithstanding a sinner's fair promises and purposes to repent, and turn to God, by these he is hindered of putting any thing into practice, but procrastinates and puts off from one time to another, until, perhaps, time is at an end, before he hath done any thing in order to his eternal salvation.

But a christian, that is fully and firmly resolved to dedicate himself to the Lord and his service, so that the whole frame of his heart is bent that way, he is so far from delaying and putting off, from one time to another, that he is ever restless, and can find no contentment in any thing he enjoys, until he has got an interest in Christ, until he has got some assurance of the love of God and the pardon of his sin: it grieves him to the very heart, to think that he should be so wild and foolish, and to waste so much of his precious time, as he has done in the fleshly lusts, in abusing God's mercy and goodness, and grieving his Spirit, in that he has made a good and gracious God wait upon him so many years, whilst he continued to run on in a course of rebellion against him. And therefore now he resolves, through the grace o God assisting him, from this time forward, to bid as everlasting farewell to his beloved sin: he now fully resolves to continue no longer in that sinful course of life; he is ready to cry out with St. Augustine, How long shall I say, to-morrow, to-morrow? Why shall not this day be the day of my conversion? He therefore without delay sets about the work of conversion; he now begins to labour, and strives to work out his salvation....

    A christian's resolution is a settled and deliberate resolution. He doth not, as many do, take up sudden and inconsiderate resolutions to follow Christ, but he diligently considers,

    1. What it may cost him to be a thorough christian; the death of his beloved sin, he knows it must cost him; he knows he must part with every sin, even with his most flesh pleasing sin, for Christ, or else he can be no christian: And he considers that it must cost him the loss of his credit and good name, his liberty, nay the loss of life itself.

    Now, a penitent sinner considers diligently of all things before he enters upon his christian course, lest after he has gone far with Christ, persecution come, and he apostatize and fall away, and so his latter end be worse than his beginning: *What man*, saith our Saviour, *intending to build a tower, sitteth not down first, and counteth the cost, whither he has sufficient to finish it, lest hapy after he has laid the foundation, and is not able to finish it, all that behold it begin to mock him,* Luke 14:28, 29. *So whosoever forsaketh not all that he hath, cannot be my disciple,* ver. 33. Many have gone far with Christ, so far as their interest lay with the interest of Christ; but when the interest of Christ and their own interest is crossed, then they have apostatized and fell away. But on the contrary, a wise christian, before he enters upon a new life, first sits down and counts the cost; he considers on Peter, how sadly he fell when Christ had left him unto himself, notwithstanding his strong resolutions, saying, *If all should deny thee, yet will not I.* Therefore he dares not purpose and resolve in his own strength,; for he knows himself to be very weak, and cannot move one step towards heaven without divine assistance; then he is day and night in earnest prayer to God, for strength from heaven; and so in strength of Christ he is resolved to run all hazards with him: he is resolved to venture all for him; to venture the loss of a good name, the loss of liberty, and the loss of life itself: as he expects to reign with Christ, so he resolves to choose him with all his offices, as a prophet to instruct him as a Saviour to save him from sin, as well as from punishment; he is resolved to cut off his right hand sins, and pluck out his right eye sins; he is resolved to spare no sin; but to strive against it, to watch against it, and fight against it with all his might; he is resolved to follow Christ thro' all difficulties and dangers, thro' sufferings and persecutions, thro' life and death, until he comes to reign with Christ in glory.

Thus have I done with the first thing considerable, what the resolution of a christian is; I must be very brief in what follows.

II. The reason of the necessity of this resolution. Now for a christian to make a settled and firm resolution is very necessary.

1. Because that until a man sets a firm and full resolution to turn to God, he is in a ready way to fall by every temptation, he is apt to put off and delay his repentance from time to time; he is still liable to give himself more and more liberty to all kind of wickedness, to let the bridle loose to his lust: nay, until a man comes into a full and settled resolution, he lies in the ready road to open prophaneness, and to the neglect of God, and holy duties. But when a man comes to a resolved point, when the whole frame and bend of his heart is set towards Christ and holiness, then there will appear earnest endeavours after the thing resolved upon. This was the resolution of *Job*, Job 31:1. *I made a covenant with mine eyes, why then should I think upon a maid?* As if he had said, *I have resolved and made a covenant with myself, as much as in me lies to avoid all temptation of sin, why then should I run myself into temptation?* Ps. 39:3. *I said, I will take heed in my ways, that I offend not with my tongue, I will keep my mouth with a bridle.*

2. This settled and firm resolution is necessary to repentance. A man may do many things in order to a work of conversion, yet if he has not a settled and

firm resolution to turn to God, he might as well do nothing; but when once a man comes to set up a settled, firm, sincere and hearty resolution to cleave fully and wholly to the Lord, and to resign up all the faculties of his soul to him, then the work is more than half done. All the other duties of Christianity will seem easy and pleasant. David resolved and swore, and therefore he would perform: *I have sworn,* saith he, *and therefore will perform, that I will keep thy statutes.* Ps. 119:106.

This much for the doctrinal part: I shall be very short in the application.

There is but one use that I shall make of this point, and that shall be a use of exhortation: it is to, that whatever the people of *Israel* did, *Joshua* was resolved that he and his house would serve the Lord.

In the first place make a firm resolution, to give up yourselves to the Lord and his service; let the men of this world do what they please, if they will not be reformed, let them take their course; if they are so in love with hell and damnation, so that they will run headlong thither, let them take their course.

But my dear friends, into whose hands this little book shall come, do you sincerely resolve to give yourselves up to the Lord, and his service; if others will be for hell, do you resolve to be for heaven; whatever it cost you, resolve to cleave close to the Lord, in opposition to the malice of the devil, the enticements of the flesh, and the temptations of this wicked world. If wicked men should entice and seek to draw you into sin with them, do not yield, but rather answer them as *Joseph* did his mistress, *How can I do this great wickedness and sin against God?* Gen. 39:9. If at any time any of your old sinful companions do entice, persuade, and intreat you to go with them to drinking, gaming, or any other vile exercises, resolve with yourselves never to yield to any of their persuading arguments; labour to obey the counsel of *Solomon; My son, if sinners entice thee, consent thou not.*

     Resolve to take Christ in all his offices, in all his inconveniences, resolve to run all hazards with him; be exhorted now, without delay, to bid an everlasting farewell to all your sins; and from henceforth make a firm covenant with thy body and soul to be his, saying, Lord, I do here lament, and am heartily grieved that I have spent so much of my time in rebellion against thee, and in chusing the ways of sin, but I do here, from this time forward, firmly resolve to bid an utter defiance to all sin, and through they grace enabling me now to covenant with thee to be thine, and to forsake all that is near and dear unto me in this world, for thy sake; I am resolved never more to yield myself servant to sin and satan but to watch against all temptations, whether of prosperity or adversity, and I do resolve to take thee for my portion and happiness, promising and vowing to serve thee in holiness and righteousness all the days of my life; and I do here fully resolve to choose Jesus Christ as the way to the Father, and to take my lot with, and to run all hazards with him, resting upon him alone, in his way for salvation.

Secondly, Resolve not only to give up yourselves to the Lord, but resolve to use your utmost endeavours, that all under your charge may likewise serve the Lord: *Joshua* did not only resolve to serve the Lord himself, but he resolved both he and his should serve the Lord….

To conclude: You that are parents, masters, and householders, if ever you desire your own good, and a blessing upon your families and undertakings, and the good of this nation, be entreated now to hear the word of exhortation; be exhorted now, no longer to neglect the worship and service of God in your families, but as often as you see your servants and children sin against God, reprove them, and when you see them ignorant, instruct them….

Excerpted from
Early Days in the Society of Friends,
Exemplifying The Obedience of Faith, in Some of its First Members
by Mary Ann Kelty
London: Harvey and Darton, 1840.

(An excerpt from the Introductory Chapter)

"We walk by faith," says the apostle, "and not by sight;" (2 Cor. 5:7) Now, the obedience which results from the walk of faith, differs from that which merely springs from attention to an *external* rule, in the same way as the motions of an automaton differ from those of a living man.

For, as the automaton, by means of certain springs, may imitate some of the actions of a living man; so, by adhering to certain religious precepts, may the obedience which is required from the creature to the Creator, be partially represented also. But, as in the case of the automaton, the *nature* of the living man cannot possibly in any measure be obtained by the means used; so neither in that of the obedience which is produced only by the sight of a rule, can the least degree of the *love* of a child of God exist; and it can require but little reasoning to demonstrate, that it is *love* alone which can give life, power, and acceptableness, to any act of duty. That husband, or father, or master of a family, whose will was obeyed by wife, children, or servants, not because they loved him, but because it was their interest to yield him obedience, and who gave it according to the measure and kind, which written regulations from him, stipulated as his right; such an one, we say, would have small occasion to congratulate himself upon their services; seeing how devoid they were of the lovely and endearing nature which can alone give value to any obedience.

"Love is the fulfilling of the law;" and love to God is no *natural* feeling; assuredly it is not born with us; neither is it a thing to be *acquired*, "If a man would give all the substance of his house for love, it would utterly be contemned," (Sol. Song, 8:7.) Love, in short, is a *living* thing--"God is love"--and God is life--eternal life--and it is by this *living* principle of *love,* that such an obedience as is acceptable to the Creator, and profitable to the creature, can *alone* be wrought out.

We must have the divine life then, before we can perform the functions of it. The *natural* will not reach to the *super*-natural. We may love our friends and kindred with such a love as fallen humanity is capable of; but to love God, we must have a new and a divine nature, since like can only have affinity with like; and hence the indispensable necessity of our being born again. "Except a man be born again," says the Saviour, "he *cannot* see the kingdom of God." The question is not whether he wishes it or not; he *cannot*--his present condition, as an unregenerate man, renders it *impossible.*

Now, as it is clear to demonstration, that life wherever it exists, is always evolved out of its own proper germ, are we to suppose that the divine life, (of which we must be born, and of which our Lord speaks, in John, 3.) is an *exception* to this universal law?--Is it said, "We must be born again, not of corruptible seed, but of incorruptible," (I Pet. 1:23,) and yet that there exists not in our fallen nature any portion of this incorruptible seed?

The scriptures do no warrant such an assumption; on the contrary, they repeatedly testify to its presence in the soul. Various names they give to it: such as "the word of the kingdom;" the "word nigh in the heart;" "the ingrafted word which is able to save the soul;" "the voice of the good Shepherd," & c.--but that by which its full sufficiency and appointed office is the most frequently exhibited, appears to be that of *light*."

"That was the true light which lightest every man that cometh into the world." (John 1.9)

"But all things that are reproved are made manifest by the light; for whatsoever doth make manifest is light."

"Wherefore he saith, awake thou that sleepest, and arise from the dead; and Christ shall give thee light." (Eph. 5:13, 14)

And who is there, it may be confidently asked, that has not, at times, been made deeply sensible of the presence of this "true light" in his soul, manifesting there the darkness and disorder of the passions, and with "a still small voice," calling upon him to renounce their Egyptian slavery?

Who is there that can be considered as serious in thought or feeling, that has not had cause to rejoice in obeying the evil of this inward illuminator? And who, that has faithfully followed *as far as* it has pleased to lead him, but has found it to be a deliverer from sin, and a "guide into all truth?"

Let all those who question its power in this respect, *first* answer to their own consciences, how *often* and how *sincerely* they have submitted to its yoke, and borne its burden, before they venture to decide upon its *not* being that incorruptible seed of the kingdom of God, of which, and into which, they are to be born again.

"I am come a light into the world," says the Redeemer thereof, "that whosoever believeth on me should not abide in darkness." Again he says, "if ye believe not that I am he, ye shall die in your sins."

Now, dear reader, what is it to believe in Jesus Christ? A question which may be answered by another: What is it to believe in anything spiritual? What is it to believe in love, joy, peace, long-suffering, gentleness, goodness, faith, meekness, temperance? Is it not to be sensible, and *feelingly conscious* of the blessed nature of these heavenly fruits? Can these divine qualities be even understood, unless the affections are in some degree partakers of their character? And *how*, or *where*, is their power to be felt, but *in the heart,* that desert land, which their presence makes to "blossom as the rose?"

    The fact then is, that we can no otherwise have faith in Jesus Christ, "the light of the world," but as we *know* the power of his life-giving spirit revealed *in our own souls.* We may read *descriptions* of this divine life, and we may desire to possess it; but if we seek for it in this or the other "outward observation," we are but wandering from the point, and spending ourselves in taking profitless steps, which all must be retraced, and our fugitive souls brought home, to sweep the house *of the heart,* and look for the lost piece of silver *there*--or it never will be found.

    In no other way can that obedience which befits a child, be born; for, in no other way can the "obedience of faith" result. We must *know* in whom we have believed; we must have *proved* the *nature* of that Being to whom we can unhesitatingly, and with loving confidence, resign ourselves. "Therefore thus saith the Lord God, behold I lay in Zion for a foundation, a stone, a tried stone, a precious corner-stone, a sure foundation:" and everlastingly true is it, that those who have built their house upon this rock, have found, upon their own experience, that the stone which the builders in every age of the church have rejected, is nevertheless, "the head of the corner."

Excepted form
Natural Goodness: or, Honour to Whom Honour is Due
By Rev. T. F. Randolph Mercein, MA
Fifth Edition. New York: Carton & Porter, 1854, pp. 63-76

Thomas Fitz Randolph Mercein, 1825-1856, was a licensed preacher of the Methodist Episcopal Church.

  We may say with accuracy sufficient, that morality consists in the observance of those duties which a man owes to others and to himself; and which are announced to him either by the voice of revelation, or by the moral sense within him, in view of the relations in which he is placed. But it will give more definiteness to our present argument to analyze morality into its several departments, and to observe the nature and peculiar rewards of several of the separate moralities.
  There is, for instance, a physical morality. The word of God, in specific language, or in implied direction, commands a life of temperance in food and beverage, a strict restraint upon the licentious appetites, regular industry and labour, cleanliness of person and apparel, and observance of frequent days of rest. The general moral sense of mankind has given to most of these rules an independent sancti0n. Now, although the result of such physical morality is not the sole object of its injunction in Scripture, nor are all the consequences clearly foreseen, where the

unaided moral sense enjoins it; yet the sure tendency of such observances is to bring the entire body to that state were all its parts of blood and bone and muscle, of sensitive nerve and organic functions, are fitted in their separate and mutual action to give the frame its highest power of strength and endurance, and fitness for all the peculiar purposes of its existence: and in the mere physical consciousness of this healthful existence, there is a physical happiness. It is not merely the absence of pain and uneasiness, but a positive feeling of buoyancy and exhilaration. And just in proportion as those laws are not observed, there is a corresponding loss of their physical rewards, and a gradual sinking into positive suffering and disease. "Even as we walk the streets we meet with illustrations of each extreme. Here behold a patriarch, whose stock of vigor threescore years and ten seem hardly to have impaired. His erect form, his firm step, his elastic limbs, and undimmed senses, are so many certificates of good conduct; or, rather, so many jewels and orders of nobility with which nature has honored him for his fidelity to her laws. His fair complexion shows that his blood has never been corrupted; his pure breath, that he has never yielded his digestive apparatus for a vintner's cess-pool; his exact language and keen apprehension, that his brain has never been drugged or stupefied by the poisons of distiller or tobacconist. Enjoying his powers to the highest, he has preserved the power of enjoying them. Despite the moral of the school-boy's story, he has eaten his cake and still kept it. As he drains the cup of life, there are no lees at the bottom. His organs will reach the goal of existence together. Painlessly as a candle burns down in its socket, so will he expire; and a little imagination would convert him into another Enoch, translated from earth to a better world without the sting of death.

"But look at an opposite extreme, where an opposite history is recorded. What wreck so shocking to behold as the wreck of a dissolute man: the vigor of life exhausted, and yet the first steps in an honorable career not taken; in himself a lazar-house of diseases; dead, but by a heathenish custom of society not buried! Rogues have had the initial letter of the title burnt into the palms of their hands. Even for murder, Cain was only branded on the forehead; but over the whole person of the debauchee, or the inebriate, the signatures of infamy are written. How nature brands him with stigma and opprobrium! How she hangs labels all over him, to testify her disgust at his existence, and to admonish others of his example! How she loosens all his joints, sends tremors along his muscles, and bends forward his frame, as if to bring him upon all-fours with kindred brutes, or to degrade him to the reptile's crawling! How she disfigures his countenance, as if intent upon obliterating all traces of her own image, so that she may swear she never made him! How she pours sheum over his eyes, sends foul spirits to inhabit his breath, and shrieks, as a trumpet, for every pore of his body, 'BEHOLD A BEAST!'" (from Horace Mann's "Thoughts for a Young Man.")

Such, then, are the rewards and the retributions

which sanction a physical morality.

There is an intellectual morality--a morality not yet comprehended as such by society, and not specifically commanded in the word of God, because its full exercise or rejections is only possible in those advanced states of civilization and freedom upon which the race has scarcely entered; but a morality destined yet to take its place beside the recognized duties of man, and urge its claims as forcibly, and with as palpable sanctions as even physical virtue. Careful observation, sober thought, close application in study, truthfulness in argument, indulgence of the fancy only as it may sweep through space as the satellite of reason--these will be some of the injunctions in the Decalogue of that new morality. And it will have its reward: the quick, clear perception, accurate and ready memory, sound judgment, clearness and reach of logic, and the chastened imagination that, like heaven's light, tints with ethereal colouring the blade, and the ear, and the full corn of thought, and crows fertility with beauty.

But there is a social morality, recognized from the beginning. The commandments of the second table of the Decalogue, explained by the sermon on the mount; the dictates of that social justice which reverences the rights of others in person, or estate, or character, and the minuter and less definable duties, revealed by the diviner radiance that beams forth when Justice is transfigured into Love; the palpable and direct applications of these great principles, and the observance of those legislative enactments, and conventional rules, which tend to secure the general peace and prosperity: such are the obligations which social morality lays upon the citizen, the man of business, the philanthropist, and the friend. Its rewards areas generous as its retribution is terrible. Respectability, commercial credit, honour, the courtesies of life, sympathy in misfortune, kindness from those we love. Each moralist reaps a larger share of happiness than he individually gives. Each heart and the life in a community, being like a burnished reflector, which, having its proper position and polish, gives its light to the common stock, but gathers a larger radiance from every other; and which, being displaced and tarnished, gives but little, and gathers less. The transgressor lives in a dark atmosphere of legal penalty and commercial distrust, of friendlessness and shame.

There is also a domestic morality--of which we speak separately, because we find it, more than any other, exercised without reference to other duties. Conjugal fidelity, parental tenderness, filial reverence and affection, and fraternal love--how human nature has felt their beauty and their sanctity, even where religion has not yet thrown over them her holier loveliness! And they have their reward. Amid the sheltering care of the domestic circle, a sacred joy springs up, like a pure spring beneath the clustering palm-trees, an oasis green and cheerful, a retreat and compensation, amid all the heat and conflict of surrounding deserts. The music of happy voices encircling our firesides and our tables--the smile of greeting--the sympathy in sorrow--the nameless little kindnesses that sparkle off from the altar of family affection--the unwearied watching of the sick chamber--and the soft arm of latest devotion, which soothes and sustains us, and aids us to lean securely upon the rod and the staff which now alone can comfort us through the shadow: all these are but the responsive blessings to that love, and care, and gentleness, which we have shown our households--the natural reward of a true domestic morality.

Once more: we may speak of a morality of the passions, apart from actual intercourse and observation by others. It is a Scriptural duty to rule our own spirits, to cultivate the generous sentiments, to repress the malevolent impulses, and to check even the necessary instincts of resentment and justice within due moderation. Now, apart from the fact that in a well-regulated social state, the gratification of the vindictive passions is most commonly debarred, and the evil affection suffers the pang of disappointment, it has been clearly shown that as each generous and noble impulse, whether it shall succeed or not in its aims, has in itself a sweetness like the glow of a healthful frame, so the malignant passions, however they may be gratified, have a constitutional misery, as a frenzied drunkard grasps the cup amid the tortures of his delirium. "Anger, wrath, malice, envy," like vipers nestling in the bosom, sting the breast that cherishes them, however shut in from outward victims. And, on the other hand, there is no loftier consciousness vouchsafed to the moralist, than to feel his mastery of himself--that his soul is not like a dismantled bark, borne away by every wind and current, but has in itself a controlling power, and, by an internal force, breasts them at its will.

Now we have glanced thus hastily at these several moralities, not to see what they were in themselves, but to call attention to the fact of their *independence* of each other; and that, existing thus separately, no one can be inferred from the existence of the other. You cannot judge the social character from business habits, nor the intellectual culture from the comparative physical health, nor domestic virtue from public amenity. The banker who never yet failed to discharge his obligations, even when financial ruin threatened, and all around were faithless, may go home to a wife, whose heart his coldness has broken, and to children, who, lost to all reverence, regard his life only as the obstacle to their enjoyment of his fortune. The most amiable and loving of parents, may have no integrity nor credit. In some cases, and to some extent, the moralities may be necessary to each other, and so be involved; as when some physical laws may be observed, to secure mental vigor, or when public moralities are observed through love and consideration for those at home. But we shall be safe in laying down the general principle, that these moralities are independent, and therefore the existence of one cannot be argued from the presence of another; that, at all events, the higher cannot be inferred from the presence of the lower moralities; and that, as they *may* and *do* occur separately, their existence all together cannot argue any connexion of principle.

And, as these *moralities* are distinct, so are their *rewards* separate. Each bears its own fruit, and each fruit crowns its own tree. The reward of domestic morality is no evidence of public esteem and confidence. So far is physical temperance, and its results, from betokening social morality, that the robust frame thus produced may only call for heavier manacles, and a stronger gibbet. The rewards of all the lower excellences, therefore, cannot argue the existence, nor the reward, of the highest. It is as though each virtue stood upon a separate pedestal, and was crowned with a separate wreath. All but one may stand erect, and their crown witness their approval by the Judge: yet neither these perfect statues, nor their crowns, prove that the noblest of them all may not lie besides them, prostrate and crownless in the dust.

Now, in view of these facts, may we not say, that if there should be added a new department of our being, or a new circle of relationship should gather around us, higher than any yet mentioned, so that there would be a new morality, the same rules would hold? Whether it in any way involved the lower moralities or not, they would not prove its existence, nor would *their* reward prove *its* reward. Just as all but one of the common moralities cannot imply that highest virtue which remains, so all earthly moralities would not prove the existence of the added excellence and duties, nor all earthly blessings guarantee the new reward.

Now, we aver that there is such a distinct and loftier morality, with its distinct reward. The soul has relations to a God, as personal in being, as definite in his attributes, as any finite soul; and the duties due to him are as palpable as those of any earthly relationship. It needs no argument to prove the profusion and exuberance of his bestowments, the ceaselessness and minuteness of his services, and the benevolence, the compassion, the forbearance, and the tenderness, of the great heart of God; nor need we dwell upon the responsive affection and services which we owe to him. If filial affection be a duty; if ingratitude is detestable; if reverence for the good be incumbent upon all; and if implicit obedience to law, which, with far-seeing wisdom, provides for the common welfare, be indispensable to true morality; then do our relations to the great Father of all spirits, to the Benefactor who makes both nature and human generosity to be but the almoners of his large bounty, to the Holy One and Just, to the Lawgiver whose unerring wisdom guides his perfect love--then do our relations to Him call for as ceaseless reverence, and love, and gratitude, and for as ceaseless embodiment of those feelings in active service, as any earthly morality. The acknowledgment of our felt dependence and indebtedness, in prayer and praise; the careful study of revelation, and of providential openings, as intimations of His command or wish; the glad consecration of time, and thought, to the filial communion of spirit with Spirit; and the minute watchfulness over all that may meet his favour or rebuke--these constitute a distinct morality. Those classes of obligations which we have before discussed, regard the soul in its relations to the world, or to itself alone: this regards its relations to God. Those human duties may seem to be demanded by conscience, even if there were no God: this higher morality, in all its essential elements of feeling and expression, would abide, in imperious obligation, although all associated existence were blotted out, and but one heart was left alone with God in his universe. Lower duties regard man in his relations to material, visible, and changing circumstances, and may be called the temporal morality: this regards the soul in its relations to God the Spirit, and to the spiritual world, and may be termed the spiritual morality. Now, it observance may require the observance of the temporal, even as we saw physical morality to be practiced for the sake of mental vigor; but as the physical does not prove the intellectual, nor the social the domestic virtues, nor all *but* the highest combined demonstrate the highest of the temporal moralities to exist; so they all, and much less a few of them, cannot demonstrate the presence of the distinct and superior spiritual morality.

    And as the moralities are distinct, so are their rewards. The earthly bring earthly blessings; the spiritual, a spiritual recompense. So far, of course, as the great morality implies the observance of the lower, it secures their natural results; but its own peculiar benefits are distinct, and not implied by them. The approving love of God, the sweet manifestation of his presence, his strength and consolations, the conscious assimilation to his character--the fulness of exceeding great and precious promises, bringing a peace that passeth understanding, and a love that passeth knowledge--these are some of those spiritual benefits which yield the highest happiness of which human nature is capable. Now, therefore, as all other moralities in no way imply this loftier excellence, neither do their rewards imply the guarantee of this loftier recompense. When these earthly rewards, and their virtuous acts, and the relationships which called them forth, have passed away, the question of *eternal morality* and *eternal rewards* will stand, as it does to-day, alone--to be determined by its own evidences.

      Thus do we find ourselves led by this hasty glance at the common morality and its rewards, as seen everywhere around us, to the conclusion, that WHATEVER THE TEMPORAL BLESSING AND CURSE, WHICH ATTEND HUMAN ACTION MAY INDICATE, IT CERTAINLY DOES NOT INDICATE ANY SUCH REGARD FOR THE MORALIST AS SHALL SECURE HIM FROM ETERNAL PUNISHMENT IN THE FUTURE WORLD.

Excerpt from an Address Delivered by Frederick Beasly, D. D., Provost of the University of Pennsylvania, to the Senior Class of the Students, on the 22d of July, 1821

As found in Jesse Torrey, Jr., The Moral Instructor and Guide to Virtue Being A Compendium of Moral Philosophy in Eight Parts. Philadelphia: Kimber and Sharpless, 1824, pp. 255-258

MY YOUNG BRETHREN,

Your intentions, are, no doubt, at this time upright, and all your views laudable.--The evil propensities and passions which are common to your race, you must be presumed to possess, but they have not yet gained the ascendancy over you better powers. If vicious inclinations have occasionally transported you into excess, this excess has been speedily succeeded by remorse and penitence, which have operated as an immediate corrective of such evil.

Whatever may have been the follies or vices, into which you may have been hurried, habits of irregularity and excess are not yet contracted, and evil propensities have not subjected you to their dominion. From your commerce with a corrupt world, and exposure to the allurements of its pleasures, and its temptations to dishonor, you have not yet relaxed your principles or tainted your morals.

If you are beginning to lisp the language of profanity, a delicate and sensitive conscience gives you warning of the outrage you are committing against God. If you have given way to the impulses of unbridled passions, the pangs of contrition have been their bitter fruits. At the prospect of shame, dishonor and infamy, your spirits would shudder within you.

Not only are you free, as yet, from the slavery of sinful passions, but the virtuous principles of your constitution, aided by the holy spirit of God, maintain a decided preponderance over those which incline you to evil. Your heart dilates with secret emulation and delight, when you have recounted any generous and noble deeds which have been performed by others. Your moral feelings are alive in all the claims of duty.

The doctrines of the gospel interest and touch your heart, while its moral precepts recommend themselves by an irresistible evidence to your understandings. You cannot walk abroad and contemplate the wonders of creation, without feeling a sacred glow of gratitude and love to their beneficent Author.

Such, at this time, my young brethren, in all probability, is your moral condition, and such are your views, feelings and principles of action. It is a happy and most precious moment of your lives, could you but be rendered sensible of its full importance. This is to you emphatically the accepted time, this is the day of salvation.

From the days of infancy to those of boyhood,

and from those of boyhood to those of youth, no determinate plans are formed, and scarcely ever any definite character impressed upon the mind.--Through this portion of the journey of life, almost all of us pass with equal thoughtlessness and frivolity, and when arrived at youth find ourselves at the same stage pursuing the same road.

Not so, however, when we have attained to youth and man hood. From the moment in which you commence on intercourse with the world on your own account, and mingle amongst its actors, entering into its interests, its sympathies and its conflicts, the paths in which you walk begin to diverge from each other. Some of them will lead you to respectability, peace, honor, fame, immortality; while others will conduct you in a downward course to shame, disgrace, misery and everlasting contempt.

You stand, my young brethren, upon the point from which this divergence begins.--Does it not infinitely concern you to give heed to the steps which you shall take next, to pause seriously, reflect and deliberate before you precipitate yourselves into unseen dangers, and begin to contest with enemies with whose strength and wiles you are unacquainted?

Hitherto amidst the levity and heedlessness of younger years, reflection and seriousness were more difficult to be attained b you; but it is now time, that you should be susceptible of the impressions of truth and duty, and should imbibe the lessons of wisdom and sobriety.

It is fearful to reflect upon the changes which

often take place in the fortunes and conditions of young men, immediately after that period of life to which you have now attained. How many opening prospects of youth are soon clouded or sunk in perpetual night! How many hearts of parents and friends are wrung with anguish at the sudden disappointment of those hopes which they had long and fondly cherished!

    You yourselves are entirely unapprised of the severity of that trial to which you must be subjected in making your way through the world--what evil communications will essay to corrupt your good manners. What blasphemies and impieties will incessantly assail your ear and insinuate a secret poison into your hearts!

    And it is to be remarked as an awful admonition, on this head, that the progress which our unruly appetites and passions make towards subjecting us to their despotism, is imperceptible; and that the demands which they make upon us are increased by every indulgence which we grant them. We are subjected to their yoke before we are aware; and then, of all the criminal desires, it may be truly said, that increase of appetite doth grow by the very aliment they have fed upon.

    How precious, in this point of light, is the period of youth, and how infinitely important the restraining influence of religion, to save it from the miseries it may bring upon itself!

    My young brethren, you may now be awake to every virtuous and noble sentiment, and susceptible of the tenderest impressions of religion--and yet, a little familiarity with scenes of guilt, may diminish your sensibility in this respect, gradually harden your heart, and vitiate your thoughts and principles of action.

Vice insidiously spreads its contamination through the youthful mind; and when once it is deeply imbibed, where is the antidote that shall check its fatal progress?--What an impressive lesson does this consideration teach you, to cultivate an early piety, which is the only effectual expedient by which you shall be saved from the evils to come!

The next consideration which should lead you to seek the grace of early piety, is, that it furnishes you with the best provision for a long and happy life.

But if virtue has sometimes to encounter persecutions and be tested by its trials, it never fails ultimately to contribute to our welfare, and promote our true enjoyment. Vice, on the other hand, by the tumult and inquietude which it awakes in the bosom, never fails, not only to imbitter our pleasures, but also to abridge the term of our present lives.

The wicked shall not live out half their days.--Intemperance, debauchery, avarice, inordinate ambition, revenge, all the wild and lawless passions, hurry their victims to untimely graves. Do you not perceive that righteousness exalteth to honor, but that sin sinketh down to shame? Are not the good, although not always, yet, for the most part, the prosperous upon earth?

Do they not find that while the name of the wicked is allowed to rot in public estimation, a good name is to them better than great riches, and loving favor than silver and gold?

Their meekness and gentleness of disposition conciliate the esteem and affection of others,--their soft words extinguish wrath,--their patience and forbearance under provocations and injuries disarm resentment and revenge,--their blameless lives and scrupulous integrity attract universal confidence,--their habitual intercourse with God, both by internal and external acts of homage, purifies their minds from all unholy desires, and quells the turbulence of unruly passions, while that ardent love of mankind which springs out of the pure fountain of religion in the heart, prompts them to those benevolent, humane and disinterested exertions, which never fail to reward the performers of them with the gratitude and attachment of their fellow-men.

"The Threefold Satisfaction of the Conscience"
from The Foundations of the Christian Faith by Charles W. Rishell
Vol. IX.--The Foundations of the Christian Faith
New York: Eaton & Mains, 1899, pp. 577-581

Note: Charles Wesley Rishell, 1850-1908, served as Professor of Historical Theology in Boston University School of Theology.

The third of the fundamental religious and ethical needs of the individual (after a satisfactory conception of God and of man) is satisfaction for his conscience. This need is threefold. (a It involves a perfect yet flexible moral standard; (b Release from the burdening sense of guilt; (c Power for righteousness, or power to resist temptation from within and from without, and to fulfill all duty.

(a The conscience can never rest in the thought of anything but the morally perfect. A standard which appears imperfect it at once rejects. With regard to this standard conscience does ot ask whether it is attainable. What it demands is an ideal upon which no apparent improvement can be made. Conscience takes such delight in this ideal that sometimes the mind is rendered forgetful of the chasm between it and actual attainment; but whatever the ideal be, if it be regarded perfect, the soul delights in it. The cry of the psalmist, "O how I love thy law! it is my meditation all the day," (Psa. 119: 97), is the expression of all morally earnest souls. Now, it is plain that this standard must also be flexible. No set of rules, no collection of precepts, can cover all the situations in which one is liable to be placed; and if such a code were possible the conscience could take no delight in it, since it would be a foreign product, and so cumbersome in its application as to be a perpetual tax on the memory and judgment. In order to be satisfactory it must be simple, and it can be simple only by being flexible.

    It scarcely need be said that Christianity in its law of love furnishes this perfect and perfectly flexible moral standard. It is a law which can be employed and applied on all occasions without unduly taxing the mind. The principal thing is that one should have and constantly maintain the purpose to fulfill the royal law according to the commandment (James 2:8). Such a purpose is love, and love is the fulfilling of the law (Rom. 13:10). It is impossible for the mind to conceive any expression of the relations of moral beings higher than that of love as taught and exemplified by Jesus Christ, nor better adapted to all races of men and every exigency of life, whether individual or social. Here again, then, Christianity meets the demands of the final form of religion.

    (b However we may account for the origin of the conscience such a faculty exists in all human beings. Furthermore, all men are aware of having voluntarily done that which their moral judgment condemned, and as a result all know the pangs of an offended conscience. To all those who believe in a

God with personal moral attributes this consciousness of moral obliquity assumes the form of a consciousness of sin. But the sense of having done wrong oppresses all men, though believers in God generally have a peculiarly tender conscience since to them, especially to Christians, wrongdoing is not only a departure from the moral ideal and an injury to our fellow-men but, in addition, an offense to that loving Being to whom we owe every blessing we enjoy. It is this contradiction of the will of a wise and beneficent friend, this ingratitude for all his favors, which lends moral delinquency and obliquity much of its turpitude in the sight of the Christian. Nevertheless, all men are burdened with a sense of guilt, and the conscience cannot be at ease while this is the case. The memory of our sins haunts us by day and by night, and happiness is impossible.

Just here it is that Christianity proves itself again exactly adapted to our human needs. Any system which does not provide for forgiveness must leave men not only unhappy but without hope of attaining morally to the best of which they are capable. For the consciousness of guilt both absorbs the attention and paralyzes the moral energies. Our time and strength are spent in vain regrets, or, if we determine to escape from this unhappy condition by forgetfulness, we can do so only by silencing within ourselves the voice of the inward monitor to whose holy inspirations we have traced all the earnestness of our moral endeavor. In the one path there is misery, in the other there is obduracy.

But, it will be asked, how does pardon of sin help the case? Does not the hope of pardon tend to make men sin lightly? Is it not better to leave men in the wretchedness of their guilt in order thereby to warn them against future iniquity? Now, there doubtless are those who gain nothing from the promise of forgiveness but the ease of conscience for which all men seek. Such, however, are not the kind who would profit by being left to their misery. He who can be profited can be profited by pardon far more than by suffering. And in the Christian system the problem of pardon is not one of justice alone but of the happiness and moral development of sinners. Even were the question one merely of justice pardon would be demanded in many instances; for sin is not always the result of deliberate choice but often arises from the overwhelming power of inherited passion. As before pointed out, a God who was just, yet lacking mercy, would tend to harden men's hearts; and the spirit of gratitude for pardon is at least a loftier motive for right-doing than the fear of suffering and its influence upon the life is also far more beneficent. But if pardon is granted it must not be bestowed as the mere act of a sovereign will. Such a procedure would rob it of all its moral value in the sign of man. It would represent sin as committed against God only, and as being merely a violation of his will. He could forgive if he wished, or withhold forgiveness if that suited him better. If his forgiveness or refusal to forgive could be supposed to have any ground in his ethical nature it would be of the character of a conflict between his justice and his mercy. If he forgave it would be in spite of justice; if not, it would be regardless of his mercy. Forgiveness under the Christian scheme affords full scope for the cooperation of the most exact justice and the tenderest mercy. There is neither conflict nor compromise between them. So that God can be just and yet the justifier (pardoner) of the sinner.

The Christian scheme not only avoids all the dangers attendant upon an unforgiving system, secures to the individual all the benefits of pardon, and enables the attributes of God to exist in harmony, but it escapes the danger of minifying sin in the eyes of man, thus subverting the moral government of God. This is accomplished in two ways, both of which are essentials in the so-called plan of salvation. The first is by what God does, or rather did, through the atonement in Christ. A discussion of this doctrine is impracticable here, and we must content ourselves with the briefest statement of its relation to forgiveness (for those who wish a fuller treatment of the subject we recommend The Atonement in Christ, by John Miley, New York and Cincinnati, 1879). The death of Christ was God's protest against sin, and expressed the fact that it cannot be committed without suffering. Nevertheless, the sufferings of Christ were not intended as a full equivalent for the sufferings sinners deserve. Rather were they a governmental expedient. They called all men's attention to the fact that God hates sin, though he forgives it. God's justice, which is not an abstract, unrelated quality, but an administrative attribute, having to do with his relation to man, not only as a sinner, but as a moral possibility, is thereby satisfied. Since, though it was substitution, it was not an exact equivalent, it leaves room for his mercy. And since the sufferings of Christ were voluntary they did him no wrong. Then the plan, so far, provides for a most effectual protest against sin the moral effect of which is to dissuade men from its commission, while it protects God's administrative justice and yet allows him to exercise that mercy which must win men to him and to the obedience of his law.

    But as a further safeguard the plan includes man's cooperation. Man is not forgiven alone on the ground of the atonement in Christ, though this is absolutely necessary to it. There is forgiveness in no other. The divine condition is the atonement, but the human condition is faith. This again has its prerequisites. It is possible only to those who realize something of the sinfulness of sin; who abhor it in themselves and others; who seek to free themselves, not alone from its penalty, but also from its power and pollution; who have come to choose the perfect moral standard of the Gospel in preference to their own sinful propensities; who see in Jesus the embodiment of that standard and are willing to accept him as their moral and spiritual guide. When anyone is in the condition just described he will be glad to throw himself upon the mercy of God in Christ and trust in him for pardon; in other words, exercise saving faith. Penitence, repentance, faith, these all combine with the atonement to save the hardened soul from ever thinking lightly of sin and to impel him to the service of his fellow-men as the highest service of God.

Without here attempting to defend the doctrine that the sense of forgiveness realized by the soul which exercises faith is supernaturally imparted we pass on to state that, as the conditions upon which forgiveness is bestowed prevent the moral disaster which its arbitrary communication might work, the nature of the forgiveness realized also precludes it. For it does not have the effect of making us forget that we were sinners, but merely makes us realize that by the mercy of God we are in a position to start anew. At the same time our sense of shame and regret is mitigated to such an extent that they are no longer the prominent elements of our religious consciousness. We have confidence, not only in God's pardoning mercy, but also in his judgment; and we see that if he ignores the past we must do the same. We had lost not only the sense of the respect of God but our self-respect. If God is now seen to respect us we can in a proper measure respect ourselves. Besides, we see that there is something which God now requires of us. We are pardoned that we may have the consciousness of being children of God and that we may become his companions and co-laborers. Our energies must not be spent in sin, nor in regret for sin, but in uplifting men and inspiring them with the mind of Christ. Such a plan, and no other, can release us from the burdening sense of guilt and hold us at the same time to the majestic tasks which we believe God has set for us.

(c At this point, however, a new difficulty meets the morally earnest soul. He has a moral standard in which his conscience can rest satisfied, and all his violations of that standard are forgiven, but he does not feel able to live in accordance with it. There are within him unwelcome impulses toward evil conduct, and when these are excited by solicitations from without he is in danger of falling into the very sins of which he recently repented and was forgiven. This is the universal experience of those who are striving to live up to a loft moral ideal. They lack power for righteousness. They can neither resist every temptation nor stimulate themselves to the fulfillment of every duty. Here again Christianity comes to our rescue and meets one of our most urgent needs. For the conscience insists that we are censurable for this failure, however energetic the exertions of our wills, and it will never approve us as long as this symptom of moral weakness continues to exhibit itself. Our only hope is in the correction of our inward evil tendencies and in the fortification of our wills with the energy requisite to keep us up to the advance line of duty. Some part of this is accomplished by the development within us of a profound abhorrence of sin. But besides this there must be born within us a new affection, powerful enough to neutralize all other attractions and to hold us to the performance of positive duty in the face of all obstacles. Such a new affection is the love of God for which Christianity provides (See Chalmers' sermon on The Explosive Power of a New Affection). Love of country, family, riches, fame, and even of self, have contributed much to the heroisms and glories of human history; but the one universal love, which includes and elevates and purifies and strengthens all others, is the love of God. Men have often mistaken God's will, but the love of God never fails to produce its effects. "The love of Christ constraineth us" (2 Cor. 5:14) has been the expression of a mighty fact in the lives of hundreds of millions of human beings.

    So Christianity satisfies the conscience by its moral standard, by its release from the burdening sense of guilt, and by supplying the power needed for a holy life.

Excerpted from
"Of the Nature of Laws in General"
Commentaries on the Laws of England, In Four Books
By Sir William Blackstone
London: A. Strahan and W. Woodfall, 12th Edition, 1793, pp. 38-42

Editors note: Sir William Blackstone, 1723-1780 was an English judge whose Commentaries became the "bible" of legal instruction studied by aspiring lawyers in America thus impressing the stamp of "natural law" upon the hearts and minds of many an early American jurist including John Marshall, John Adams, and Abraham Lincoln.

Law, in its most general and comprehensive sense, signifies a rule of action; and is applied indiscriminately to all kinds of action, whether animate or inanimate, rational or irrational. Thus we say, the laws of motion, of gravitation, of optics, or mechanics, as well as the laws of nature and of nations. And it is that rule of action, which is prescribed by some superior, and which the inferior is bound to obey.

Thus when the supreme being formed the universe, and created matter out of nothing, he impressed certain principles upon that matter, from which it can never depart, and without which it would cease to be. When he put that matter into motion, he established certain laws of motion, to which all moveable bodies must conform. And, to descend from the greatest operations to the smallest, when a workman forms a clock, or other piece of mechanism, he establishes at his own pleasure certain arbitrary laws for its direction; as that the hand shall describe a given space in a given time; to which law as long as the work conforms, so long it continues in perfection, and answers the end of its formation.

If we farther advance, from mere inactive matter to vegetable and animal life, we shall find them still governed by laws; more numerous indeed, but equally fixed and invariable. The whole progress of plants, from the feed to the root, and from thence to the feed again;--the method of animal nutrition, digestion, secretion, and all other branches of vital economy; --are not left to chance, or the will of the creature itself, but are performed in a wondrous involuntary manner, and guided by unerring rules laid down by the great creator.

This then is the signification of law, a rule of action dictated by some superior being: and, in those creatures that have neither the power to think, nor to will, such laws must be invariably obeyed, so long as the creature itself subsists, for its existence depends on that obedience. But laws, in their more confined sense, ... and in which it is our present business to consider them, denote the rules, not of action in general, but of *human* action or conduct: that is, the precepts by which man, the noblest of all sublunary beings, a creature endowed with both reason and freewill, is commanded to make use of those faculties in the general regulation of his behaviour.

Man, considered as a creature, must necessarily be subject to the laws of his creator, for he is entirely a dependent being. A being, independent of any other, has no rule to pursue, but such as he prescribes to himself; but a state of dependence will inevitably oblige the inferior to take the will of him, on whom he depends, as the rule of his conduct: not indeed in every particular, but in all those points wherein his dependence consists. This principle therefore has more or less extent and effect, in proportion as the superiority of the one and the dependence of the other is greater of less, absolute or limited. And consequently, as man depends absolutely upon his maker for every thin, it is necessary that he should in all points conform to his maker's will.

This will of his maker is called the law of nature. For as God, when he created matter, and endued it with a principle of mobility, established certain rules for the perpetual direction of that motion; so, when he created man, and endued him with freewill to conduct himself in all parts of life, he laid down certain immutable laws of human nature, whereby that freewill is in some degree regulated and restrained, and gave him also the faculty of reason to discover the purport of those laws.

Considering the creator only as a being of infinite *power*, he was able unquestionably to have prescribed whatever laws he pleased to his creature, man, however unjust or severe. But as he is also a being of infinite *wisdom*, he has laid down only such laws as were founded in those relations of justice, that existed in the nature of things antecedent to any positive precept. These are the eternal, immutable laws of good and evil, to which the creator himself in all his dispensations conforms; and which he has enabled human reason to discover, so far as they are necessary for the conduct of human actions. Such among others are these principles: that we should live honestly…, should hurt nobody, and should render to every one his due; to which three general precepts Justinian has reduced the whole doctrine of law.

    But if the discovery of these first principles of the law of nature depended only upon the due exertion of right reason, and could not otherwise be obtained than by a chain of metaphysical disquisitions, mankind would have wanted some inducement to have quickened their inquiries, and the greater part of the world would have rested content in mental indolence, and ignorance it's inseparable companion. As therefore the creator is a being, not only of infinite *power,* and *wisdom,* but also of infinite *goodness*, he has been pleased so to contrive the constitution and frame of humanity, that we should want no other prompter to inquire after and pursue the rule of right, but only our own self-love, that universal principle of action. For he has so intimately connected, so inseparably interwoven the laws of eternal justice with the happiness of each individual, that the latter cannot be attained but by observing the former; and, if the former be punctually obeyed, it cannot but induce the latter. In consequence of which mutual connection of justice and human felicity, he has not perplexed the law of nature with a multitude of abstracted rules and precepts, referring merely to the fitness or unfitness of things, as some have vainly surmised; but has graciously reduced the rule of obedience to this one paternal precept, "that man should pursue his own true and substantial happiness." This is the foundation of what we call ethics, or natural law. For the several articles into which it is branched in our systems, amount to no more than demonstrating, that this or that action tends to man's real happiness, and therefore very justly concluding that the performance of it is a part of the law of nature; or, on the other hand, that this or that action is destructive of man's real happiness, and therefore that the law of nature forbids it.

This law of nature, being coeval with mankind and dictated by God himself, is of course superior in obligation to any other. It is binding over all the globe in all countries, and at all times: no human laws are of any validity, if contrary to this…; and such of them as are valid derive all their force, and all their authority, mediately or immediately, from this original.

But in order to apply this to the particular exigencies of each individual, it is still necessary to have recourse to reason: whole office it is to discover, as was before observed, what the law of nature directs in every circumstance of life; by considering, what method will tend the most effectually to our own substantial happiness. And if our reason were always, as in our first ancestor before his transgression, clear and perfect, unruffled by passions, unclouded by prejudice, unimpaired by disease or intemperance, the talk would be pleasant and easy; we should need no other guide but this. But every man now finds the contrary in his own experience; that his reason is corrupt, and his understanding full of ignorance and error.

  This has given manifold occasion for the benign interposition of divine providence; which in compassion to the frailty, the imperfection, and the blindness of human reason, hath been pleased, at sundry times and in divers manners, to discover and enforce its laws by an immediate and direct revelation. The doctrines thus delivered we call the revealed or divine law, and they are to be found only in the holy scriptures. These precepts, when revealed are found upon comparison to be really a part of the original law of nature, as they tend in all their consequences to man's felicity. But we are not from thence to conclude that the knowledge of these truths was attainable by reason, in its present corrupted state; since we find that, until they were revealed, they were hid from the wisdom of ages. As then the moral precepts of this law are indeed of the same original with those of the law of nature, so their intrinsic obligation is of equal strength and perpetuity. Yet undoubtedly the revealed law is of infinitely more authenticity than the moral system, which is framed by ethical writers, and denominated the natural law. Because one is the law of nature, expressly declared so to be by God himself; the other is only what, by the assistance of human reason we imagine to be that law. If we could be as certain of the latter as we are of the former, both would have an equal authority: but, till then, they can never be put in any competition together.

Upon these two foundations, the law of nature and the law of revelation, depend all human laws; that is to say, no human laws should be suffered to contradict these. There are, it is true, a great number of indifferent points, in which both the divine law and the natural leave a man at his own liberty; but which are found necessary for the benefit of society to be restrained with certain limits. And herein it is that human laws have their greatest force and efficacy; for, with regard to such points as are not indifferent, human laws are only declaratory of, and act in subordination to, the former.

Excerpted from
Causes of the Progress of Liberal Christianity in New England
by James Walker
Boston: Isaac R. Butts and Co., 1826, pp., 11-16.

Editor's note: James Walker, 1794-1874, was a Unitarian minister and President of Harvard College.

We do not pretend, that our fathers were free from the errors and the bigotry common to their times; but there is one thing, in which they differed from all their contemporaries, and which entitles them to the gratitude and veneration of their posterity. Though they had their errors and their bigotry, they did not seek to entail them on their descendants, by incorporating them into formularies and creeds, that were to be of perpetual obligation. They left their views of religion, such as they were; but they left them without any obstacle to their correction and amendment, whenever this should become necessary to accommodate them to the progressive illumination of the human mind. Compare our condition in this respect, with that of the English Establishment, from which our fathers separated. The liberal members of that church have eight times attempted its reform, but without the least success; so as to justify the strong language used by one of its most distinguished ornaments, as he looked back on these failures, and in the bitterness of his soul considered that the cause of them was permanent. "Here, then, hath Terminus fixed his pedestal, and here hath he kept his station for two whole centuries. We are just where the Acts of Uniformity left us, and where, for aught that appears in the temper of the times, the last trumpet will find us."

No, it will not be so. There is a power at work, stronger--infinitely stronger--than the establishments of men, which is trying all establishments, as it were, by fire. They may multip0ly their creeds and subscriptions, until, to use the language of Milton, "he who would take orders, must subscribe slave, and take an oath withal;" there is that, however in the *tendencies* of society and the human mind, which tells us that they cannot be forever resisted. But though creeds and establishments cannot stop the progress of truth, they may, and they will, obstruct its natural and regular progress; and it is because they have not existed in our churches to obstruct the natural and regular progress of truth, that Liberal Christianity has made such advances. It is remarkable of Liberal Christianity in New England, that it is almost entirely of domestic growth. It was not brought here; it has grown up spontaneously. Intelligent and thinking men all over the country, without any concert, and with nothing but the Bible for their guide, have been led to adopt liberal views; in some instances without being aware at the time, that there were any other persons in the world holding a similar faith. Nay I believe it to be undeniable, that wherever all artificial obstructions to free enquiry are removed, Liberal

Christianity will spring up spontaneously. Its friends certainly think so; and that its enemies think so too, is proved by the fact of their resorting to these artificial obstructions, avowedly as their only security against its further and universal spread. To account, therefore, for the greater progress which Liberal Christianity has made in New England, than elsewhere, it is only necessary to consider, what all will concede, that there is no other place in the world, where so few artificial obstructions exist to the progress of truth.

I have room to consider but one other cause, which has contributed to make the progress of Liberal Christianity more rapid, and more observable in New England, than elsewhere. It is to be found in the interest taken by the people generally, and especially by the thinking and intelligent part of the community, in theological discussions.

Unhappily in most other places the reading and influential classes bestow but little attention on religious inquiries; either from indifference to the whole subject, or from disgust at the forms under which they commonly hear it presented, or from an impression that these are matters to be left to the clergy for them to manage. But in New England it has always been different. From the beginning we find the governors, judges and counselors mingling with their ministers, and supporting with great ability their own views on points of doctrine and discipline. This, of course, has had the effect to elevate the standard of thought and conversation on religious subjects; and this again has stimulated the clergy to greater efforts, that they might bring their preaching up to this standard: so that two good influences have been exerted on these, also, of a kind to act and react perpetually on one another. As a general rule, the preaching in any place will be what public sentiment demands, and never much above what public sentiment demands.

There is, also, another effect, which the interest taken by the laity in theological discussions has had on the progress of religious knowledge. We find that where this subject has occupied the minds, as well as affected the hearts of laymen, their studies have commonly resulted in their embracing liberal sentiments. I might here refer, if it were necessary, to the immortal names of Newton, Milton, and Locke; who are known to have given the whole force of their prodigious powers to the investigation of religious truth, and to have rested at last in the adoption of liberal principles. I might also say the same of some of the most distinguished statesmen, and jurists, and general scholars of our own country, living and dead. Nor is it difficult to account for the fact that the religious inquiries of laymen should more frequently terminate in the adoption of liberal views, than those of the clergy; as laymen must be supposed to be more free from sectarian biases, and to have fewer personal interests to warp the judgment, perhaps unconsciously; and besides the layman derives an advantage from an intimate acquaintance with the world and human nature, which the divine with his reserved and recluse habits can hardly hope to acquire. As, therefore, there is no place in the world where the opinions of laymen have had so much influence in deciding the public mind on the subject of religion, as in New England, we cannot wonder at the prevalence it has given to Liberal Christianity. I may also be permitted to add, that as the testimony of laymen for the truth of Christianity in general, other things being equal, is admitted by all to be of more weight than the testimony of the clergy, inasmuch as the former cannot be suspected of professional leanings; so likewise their testimony for any particular form of Christianity is deserving of the more regard for the same reason.

    The truth is, that the change which has taken place in religious opinions in this quarter is owing much more to what the people have done, than to what the clergy have done. The clergy, as a body, never yet led the way in improvement, and never will. Here, as elsewhere, the people were before them, and are before them, and probably always will be before them. It is much the fashion with some men not unfriendly on the w hole to Liberal Christianity, to speak however of the change it has introduced, as a great and hazardous experiment. But who are referred to, as trying this experiment?--The clergy? If so, it is contradicted by what we have just said. Besides, it is in no proper sense an experiment, that any body is trying. It is no more an experiment, than the revival of letters was an experiment. It is no more an experiment, than the Reformation under Luther was an experiment. It is no more an experiment, than the American Revolution was an experiment. It is the natural, and I may add, the necessary consequence of an advanced state of society in every other kind of knowledge, enabling and requiring it to make a corresponding advancement in religious knowledge. It is not the work of passion or caprice, nor the influence of a few powerful individuals, nor any reconverted plan of a refined policy; but the natural and necessary result of the progress of the human mind. It is the progress of min; and this again has been carried on by the combined action of a million of causes operating together as certainly and irresistibly as the laws of nature.

Thus do I trace the rise and progress of Liberal Christianity in New England to the same general causes, to which we are also indebted for almost everything else, that distinguishes our condition as a highly favored people.

Well may we have confidence in views, that are making progress in the world by such means. And as we profess to hold doctrines, that approach nearer than any others to the instructions of our blessed Lord, let us endeavour to make our characters and our lives approach as much nearer to his example. It has long been felt that Christianity is destined, in the providence of God, to affect much more directly and powerfully the social and moral condition of mankind, than any of its forms heretofore established have evinced a capacity for doing. If we have found that form which possesses this capacity, let it appear.

Let it elevate the tone of moral feeling in the community. Let it save our youth from the pollutions of a sensual life. Let it make the conduct of our men of standing and influence more decidedly religious and christian. Let it reform and purify the public amusements, which have so much to do in forming the character of a people. Let it increase the abhorrence felt against war, and against all anti-christian practices of communities and states. Over all, and above all, let it induce a spirit of humble, ardent, and enlightened piety. Then shall be fulfilled the prediction of our fathers; that in the feeble churches, which they were planting in a strange land, there should spring up a light, such as had never dawned on the corrupt establishments of the old world. Nor will its blessed influences be confined to any kindred, or country, or tongue. But He, who ruleth in the earth, "shall destroy in this mountain the face of the covering cast over all people, and the veil that is spread over all nations."

Excerpted from
American Institutions and their Influence (Democracy in America)
by Alexis de Tocqueville
Translated into English by Henry Reeve
New York: A. S. Barnes & Co., 1856, pp. 307-312

…. The sects which exist in the United States are innumerable. They all differ in respect to the worship which is due from man to his Creator; but they all agree in respect to the duties which are due from man to man. Each sect adores the Deity in its own peculiar manner; but all the sects preach the same moral law in the name of God. If it be of the slightest importance to man, as an individual, that his religion should be true, the case of society is not the same. Society has no future life to hope for or to fear; and provided the citizens profess a religion, the peculiar tenets of that religion are of very little importance to its interests. Moreover, almost all the sects of the United States are comprised within the great unity of Christianity, and Christian morality is everywhere the same.

It may be believed without unfairness, that a certain number of Americans puruse a peculiar form of worship, from habit more than from conviction. In the United States the sovereign authority is religious, and consequently hypocrisy must be common; but there is no country in the whole world in which the Christian religion retains a greater influence over the souls of men than in America; and there can be no greater proof of its utility, and of it conformity to human nature, than that its influence is most powerfully felt over the most enlightened and free nation of the earth.

I have remarked that the members of the American clergy in general, without even excepting those who do not admit religious liberty, are all in favor of civil freedom; but they do not support any particular political system. They keep aloof from parties, and from public affairs. In the United States religion exercises but little influence upon the laws, and upon the details of public opinion; but it directs the manners of the community, and by regulating domestic life, it regulates the state.

I do not question that the great austerity of manners which is observable in the United States, arises, in the first instance, from religious faith. Religion is often unable to restrain man from the numberless temptations of fortune; nor can it check that passion for gain which every incident of his life contributes to arouse; but its influence over the mind of women is supreme, and women are the protectors of morals. There is certainly no country in the world where the tie of marriage is so much respected as in America, or where conjugal happiness is more highly or worthily appreciated. In Europe almost all the disturbances of society arise from the irregularities of domestic life. To despise the natural bonds and legitimate pleasures of home, is to contract a taste for excesses, a restlessness of heart, and the evil of fluctuating desires. Agitate by the tumultuous passions which frequently disturb his dwelling, the European is galled by the obedience which the legislative powers of the state exact. But when the American retires from the turmoil of public life to the bosom of his family, he finds in it the image of order and of peace. There his pleasures are simple and natural, his joys are innocent and calm; and as he finds that an orderly life is the surest path to happiness, he accustoms himself without difficulty to moderate his opinions as well as his tastes. While the European endeavors to forget his domestic troubles by agitating society, the American derives from his own home that love of order, which he afterward carries with him into public affairs.

In the United States the influence of religion is not confined to the manners, but it extends to the intelligence of the people. Among the Anglo-Americans, there are some who profess the doctrines of Christianity from a sincere belief in them, and others who do the same because they are afraid to be suspected of unbelief. Christianity, therefore, reigns without any obstacle, by universal consent; the consequence is, as I have before observed, that every principle of the moral world is fixed and determinate, although the political world is abandoned to the debates and the experiments of men. Thus the human mind is never left to wander across a boundless field; and, whatever may be its pretensions, it is checked from time to time by barriers which it cannot surmount. Before it can perpetrate innovation, certain primal and immutable principles are laid down, and the boldest conceptions of human device are subjected to certain forms which retard and stop their completion.

The imagination of the Americans, even in its greatest flights, is circumspect and undecided; its impulses are checked, and its works unfinished. These habits of restraint recur in political society, and are singularly favorable both to the tranquility of the people and the durability of the institutions it has established. Nature and circumstances concurred to make the inhabitants of the United States bold men, as is sufficiently attested by the enterprising spirit with which they seek for fortune. If the minds of Americans were free from all trammels, they would very shortly become the most daring innovators and the most implacable disputants in the world. But the revolutionists of America are obliged to profess an ostensible respect for Christian morality and equity, which does not easily permit them to violate the laws that oppose their designs; nor would they find it easy to surmount the scruples of their partisans, even if they were able to get over their own. Hitherto no one, in the United States, has dared to advance the maxim, that everything is permissible with a view to the interests of society; an impious adage, which seems to have been invented in an age of freedom, to shelter all the tyrants of future ages. Thus while the law permits the Americans to do what they please, religion prevents them from conceiving, and forbids them to commit, what is rash and unjust.

Religion in America takes no direct part in the government of society, but it must nevertheless be regarded as the foremost of the political institutions of that county; for if it does not impart a taste for freedom, it facilitates the use of free institutions. Indeed, it is in this same point of view that the inhabitants of the United States themselves look upon religious belief. I do not know whether all the Americans have a sincere faith in their religion; for who can search the human heart? But I am certain that they hold it to be indispensable to the maintenance of republican institutions. This opinion is not peculiar to a class of citizens or to a party, but it belongs to the whole nation, and to every rank of society.

In the United States, if a political character attacks a sect, this may not prevent even the partisans of that very sect, from supporting him; but if he attacks all the sects together, every one abandons him, and he remains alone.

While I was in America, a witness, who happened to be called at the assizes of the county of Chester (state of New York), declared that he did not believe in the existence of God or in the immortality of the soul. The judge refused to admit his evidence, on the ground that the witness had destroyed beforehand all the confidence of the court in what he was about to say…. The newspapers related the fact without any farther comment.

The Americans combine the notions of Christianity and of liberty so intimately in their minds, that it is impossible to make them conceive the one without the other; and with them this conviction does not spring from the barren traditionary faith which seems to vegetate in the soul rather than to live.

I have known of societies formed by the Americans to send out ministers of the gospel into the new western states, to found schools and churches there, lest religion should be suffered to die away in those remote settlements, and the rising states be less fitted to enjoy free institutions than the people from which they emanated. I met with wealthy new Englanders who abandoned the country in which they were born, in order to lay the foundations of Christianity and of freedom on the banks of the Missouri or in the prairies of Illinois. Thus religious zeal is perpetually stimulated in the United States by the duties of patriotism. These men do not act from an exclusive consideration of the promises of a future life; eternity is only one motive of their devotion to the cause; and if you converse with these missionaries of Christian civilisation, you will be surprised to find how much value they set upon the goods of this world, and that you meet with a politician where you expected to find a priest. They will tell you that "all the American republics are collectively involved with each other; if the republics of the west were to fall into anarchy, or to be mastered by a despot, the republican institutions which now flourish upon the shores of the Atlantic Ocean would be in great peril. It is therefore our interest that the new states should be religious, in order to maintain our liberties."

Such are the opinions of the Americans; and if any hold that the religious spirit which I admire is the very thing most amiss in America, and that the only element wanting to the freedom and happiness of the human race is to believe in some blind cosmogony, or to assert with Cabanis the secretion of thought by the brain, I can only reply, that those who hold this language have never been in America, and that they have never seen a religious or a free nation. When they return from their expedition, we shall hear what they have to say.

There are persons in France who look upon republican institutions as a temporary means of power, of wealth and distinction; men who are the *condottieri* of liberty, and who fight for their own advantage, whatever be the colors they wear: it is not to these that I address myself. But there are others who look forward to the republican form of government as a tranquil and lasting state, toward which modern society is daily impelled by the ideas and manners of the time, and who sincerely desire to prepare men to be free. When these men attack religious opinions, they obey the dictates of their passions to the prejudice of their interests. Despotism may govern without faith, but liberty cannot. Religion is much more necessary in the republic which they set forth in glowing colors, than in the monarchy which they attack; and it is more needed in democratic republics than in any others. How is it possible that society should escape destruction if the moral tie be not strengthened in proportion as the political tie is relaxed? And what can be done with a people which is its own master, if it be not submissive to the Divinity?

Excerpted from
The Life of Rev. David Brainerd, Chiefly Extracted from His Diary
by Jonathan Edwards
New York: American Tract Society, c. 1830, pp. 161-166

Editor's note: David Brainerd, 1718-1747 was thwarted in his goal of becoming a minister because of a law that forbade the appointment of ministers in Connecticut unless they were graduates of Harvard, Yale, or a European institution (Brainerd had been sent home from Yale during his second year because of being seriously ill, probably with tuberculosis). As a result, he devoted himself to missionary work among the Native Americans. His work was supported by the Society in Scotland for Propagating Christian Knowledge.

Lord's day, Aug. 25.-- "Preached in the forenoon from Luke, 15:3-7. A number of white people being present, I made an address to them at the close of my discourse to the Indians; but could not so much as keep them orderly; for scores of them kept walking and gazing about, and behaved more indecently than any Indians I have ever addressed. A view of their abusive conduct so sunk my spirits, that I could scarcely go on with my work.

"In the afternoon I discoursed from Rev. 3:20, at which time *fifteen* Indians made a public profession of their faith. After the crowd of spectators were gone I called them together, and discoursed to them in particular; at the same time inviting others to attend. I reminded them of the solemn obligations they were now under to live to God; warned them of the evil and dreadful consequences of careless living, especially after their public profession of Christianity; gave them directions for future conduct; and encouraged them to watchfulness and devotion, by setting the comfort and happy conclusion of a religious life.

"This was a desirable and sweet season indeed! Their hearts were engaged and cheerful in duty; and they rejoiced that they had, in a public and solemn manner, dedicated themselves to God. Love seemed to reign among them! They took each other by the hand with tenderness and affection, as if their hearts were knit together, while I was discoursing to them; and all their deportment toward each other was such, that a serious spectator might justly be excited to cry out with admiration, 'Behold how they love one another.' Numbers of the other Indians, on seeing and hearing these things, were much affected, and wept bitterly; longing to be partakers of the same joy and comfort which these discovered by their very countenances as well as conduct.

Aug. 26-- "Preached to my people from John, 6:51-55. After I had discoursed some time, I addressed them in particular who entertained hopes that they were passed from death unto life. Opened to them the persevering nature of those consolations which Christ gives his people, and which I trusted he had bestowed upon some in that assembly; showed them that such have already the beginnings of eternal life, and that their heaven shall speedily be completed.

"I no sooner began to discourse in this strain

than the dear Christians in the congregation began to be melted with affection to, and desire of the enjoyment of Christ, and of a state of perfect purity. They wept affectionately, yet joyfully; and their tears and sobs discovered brokenness of heart, and yet were attended with real comfort and sweetness. It was a tender, affectionate, humble and delightful meeting, and appeared to be the genuine effect of a spirit of adoption, and very far from the spirit of bondage under which they not long since labored. The influence seemed to spread from these through the whole assembly; and there quickly appeared a wonderful concern among them. Many, who had not yet found Christ as an all-sufficient Savior, were surprisingly engaged in seeking after him. It was indeed a lovely and very interesting assembly. Their number was now about *nine-five* persons, old and young, and almost all affected with joy in Christ Jesus, or with the utmost concern to obtain an interest in him.

"Being now convinced that it was my duty to take a journey far back to the Indians on the Susquehanna, it being now a proper season of the year to find them generally at home; after having spent some hours in public and private discourse with my people, I told them that I must now leave them for the present, and go to their brethren far remote, and preach to them; that I wanted the Spirit of God should go with me, without whom nothing could be done to any good purpose among the Indians--as they themselves had opportunity to see and observe by the barrenness of our meetings at some times, when there was much pains taken to affect and awaken sinners, and yet to little or no purpose; and asked them if they could not be willing to spend the remainder of the day in prayer for me, that God would go with me, and succeed my endeavors for the conversion of these poor souls. They cheerfully complied with the motion, and soon after I left them, the sun being about an hour and a half high, they began and continued praying till break of day, or very near; never mistrusting, as they tell me, till they went out and viewed the stars, and saw the morning star a considerable height, that it was later than bed time. Thus eager and unwearied were they in their devotions! A remarkable night it was; attended, as my Interpreter tells me, with a powerful influence upon those who were yet under concern, as well as those who had received comfort. There were, I trust, this day, two distressed souls brought to the enjoyment of solid comfort in Him in whom the weary find rest. It was likewise remarkable, that this day an old Indian, who had all his days been an idolater, was brought to give up his rattles, which they use for music in their idolatrous feasts and dances, to the other Indians, who quickly destroyed them. This was done without any interference of mine, I having not spoken to him about it, so that it seemed to be nothing but the power of God's word, without any particular application to this sin, that produced this effect. Thus God has begun; thus he has hitherto surprisingly carried on a work of grace among these

Indians. May the glory be ascribed to Him who is the sole author of it."

Forks of Delaware, in Pennsylvania, Sept. 1745.

Lord's day, Sept. 1-- "Preached to the Indians from Luke, 11:16-23. The word appeared to be attended with some power, and caused some tears in the assembly. Afterward preached to a number of white people present, and observed many of them in tears; and some who had formerly been as careless and unconcerned about religion, perhaps, as the Indians. Toward night discoursed to the Indians again, and perceived a greater attention, and more visible concern among them than has been usual in these parts.

Sept. 3.-- "Preached to the Indians from Isaiah, 52:3-6. The Divine presence seemed to be in the midst of the assembly, and a considerable concern spread among them. Sundry persons seemed to be awakened; among whom were two stupid creatures, whom I could scarce ever before keep awake while I was discoursing to them. I could not but rejoice at this appearance of things; although at the same time I could not but fear, lest the concern which they at present manifested might prove like a morning cloud, as something of that nature had formerly done in these parts.

Sept. 5.-- "Discoursed to the Indians from the parable of the sower. Afterward I conversed particularly with a number of persons; which occasioned them to weep, and even to cry out in an affecting manner, and seized others with surprise and concern. I doubt not but that a divine power accompanied what was then spoken. Several of these persons had been with me to Crossweeksung, and there had seen, and some of them, I trust, *felt* the power of God's word in an affecting and saving manner. I asked one of them, who had obtained comfort, and given hopeful evidence of being truly religious, 'Why he now cried?' He replied, 'When he thought how Crist was slain like a lamb, and spilt his blood for sinners, he could not help crying when he was alone;' and thereupon burst into tears and cried again. I then asked his wife, who had likewise been abundantly comforted, why she cried? She answered, 'that she was grieved that the Indians *here* would not come to Christ, as well as those at Crossweeksung.' I asked her if she found a heart to pray for them, and whether Christ had seemed *to be near her of late in prayer'*, as in times past, which is my usual method of expressing a sense of the divine presence. She replied, 'Yes, he had been near to her, and at times when she had been praying alone, her heart loved to pray so that she could not bear to leave the place, but wanted to stay and pray longer.'

Lord's day, Sept. 8. -- "Discoursed to the Indians in the afternoon from Acts, 2:36-39. The word of God at this time seemed to fall with weight and influence upon them. There were but few present; but most that were, were in tears, and several cried out in distressing concern for their souls. There was one man considerably awakened, who never before discovered any concern for his soul. There appeared a remarkable work of the Divine Spirit among them generally, not unlike what has been of late at Crossweeksung. It seemed as if the divine influence had spread thence to this place, although something of it appeared here before in the awakening of my interpreter, his wife and some few others. Several of the careless white people now present were awakened, or at least startled, seeing the power of God so prevalent among the Indians. I then made a particular address to them, which seemed to make some impression upon them, and excite some affection in them.

"There are some Indians in these parts who have always refused to hear me preach, and have been enraged against those who have attended on my preaching. But of late they are more bitter than ever; scoffing at christianity, and sometimes asking my hearers 'How often they have cried,' and 'whether they have not now cried enough to do their turn,' &c. So that they have already trial of cruel mockings.

Sept. 9.-- "Left the Indians at the Forks of Delaware, and set out on a journey toward Susquehanna river, directing my course toward the Indian town more than an hundred and twenty miles westward from the Forks. Traveled about fifteen miles and there lodged....

Excerpted from
The English Reader
by Lindley Murray
Brattleborough: Printed by W. Fessenden for Isaiah Thomas, Jun., 1805, pp. 163-170

Lindley Murray, 1745-1826, practiced law successfully in New York until the American Revolution when, as a loyalist, he was forced into exile and retirement in England. There he devoted the rest of his life to literary pursuits, writing eleven textbooks, sixteen million copies of which were sold in America and another four million copies in Britain. His most popular work, the English Reader, full of selections from liberal writers of the Scottish Enlightenment, dominated the American market for readers from 1815 well into the 1840's when it began to be replaced by the McGuffey Readers. Abraham Lincoln is said to have referred to Lindley's English Reader as "the best schoolbook ever put in the hands of an American youth."

SECTION V.
ON THE GOVERNMENT OF OUR THOUGHTS.

A MULTITUDE of cases occur, in which we are no less accountable for what we think, than for what we do.

As, first, when the introduction of any train of thought depends upon ourselves, and is our voluntary act; by turning our attention towards such objects, awakening such passions, or engaging in such employments, as we know must give a peculiar determination to our thoughts. Next, when thoughts, by whatever accident they may have been originally suggested, are indulged with deliberation and complacency. Though the mind has been passive in their reception, and, therefore, free from blame; yet if they be active in their continuance, the guilt becomes its own. They may have intruded at first, like unbidden guests; but if when entered, they are made welcome, and kindly entertained, the case is the same as if they had been invited from the beginning. If we be thus accountable to God for thoughts either voluntarily introduced, or deliberately indulged, we are no less so, in the last place, for those which find admittance into our hearts from supine negligence, from total relaxation of attention; from allowing our imagination to rove with entire license, "like the eyes of the fool, towards the ends of the earth." Our minds are, in this case, thrown open to folly and vanity. They are prostituted to every evil thing which pleases to take possession. The consequences must all be charged to our account; and in vain we plead excuse from human infirmity. Hence it appears, that the great object at which we are to aim in governing our thoughts, is, to take the most effectual measures for preventing the introduction of such as are sinful, and for hastening their expulsion, if they shalt have introduced themselves without consent of the will.

  But when we descend into our breasts, and examine how far we have studied to keep this object in view, who can tell, "how oft the hath offended?" In no article of religion or morals are men more culpably remiss, than in the unrestrained indulgence they give to fancy; and that too, for the most part, without remorse. Since the time that reason began to exert her powers, thought, during our waking hours, has been active in every breast, without a moment's suspension or pause. The current of ideas has been always flowing. The wheels of the spiritual engine have circulated with perpetual motion. Let me ask, what has been the fruit of this incessant activity with the great part of mankind? Of the innumerable hours that have been employed in thought, how few are marked with any permanent or useful effect? How many have either passed away in idle dreams; or have been abandoned to anxious discontented musings, to unsocial and malignant passions, or to irregular and criminal desires? Had I power to lay open the store house of iniquity which the hearts of too many conceal; could I draw out and read to them a list of all the imaginations they have devised, and all the passions they have indulged in secret; what a picture of men should I present to themselves! What crimes would they appear to have perpetrated in secrecy, which to their most intimate companions they durst not reveal!

    Even when men imagine their thoughts to be innocently employed, they to commonly suffer them to run out into extravagant imaginations, and chimerical plans of what they would wish to attain, or choose to be, if they could frame the course of things according to their desire. Though such employments of fancy come not under the same description with those which are plainly criminal, yet wholly unblameable they seldom are. Besides the waste of time which the occasion, and the misapplication which they indicate of those intellectual powers that were given to us for much nobler purposes, such romantic speculations lead us always into the neighborhood of forbidden regions. They place us on dangerous ground. They are for the most part connected with some one bad passion; and they always nourish a giddy and frivolous turn of thought. They unfit the mind for applying with vigor to rational pursuits, or for acquiescing in sober plans of conduct. From the ideal world in which it allows itself to dwell, it returns to the commerce of men, unbent and relaxed, sickly and tainted, averse to discharging the duties, and sometimes disqualified even for relishing the pleasures, of ordinary life. BLAIR.

SECTION VI.
ON THE EVILS WHICH FLOW FORM UNRESTRAINED PASSIONS.

When man revolted from his Maker, his passions rebelled against himself; and, for being originally the ministers of reasons, have become the tyrants of the soul. Hence, in treating of this subject, two things may be assumed as principles; first, that through the present weakness of the understanding, our passions are often directed towards improper objects; and next, that even when their direction is just, and their objects are innocent, they perpetually tend to run into excess; they always hurry us towards their gratification, with a blind and dangerous impetuosity. On these two points then turns the whole government of our passions: first, to ascertain the roper objects of their pursuit; and next, to restrain them in that pursuit, when they would carry us beyond the bounds of reasons. If there be any passion which intrudes itself unseasonably into our mind, which darkens and troubles our judgment, or habitually discomposes our temper; which unfits us for properly discharging the duties, or disqualifies us for cheerfully enjoying the comforts of life, we may certainly conclude it to have gained a dangerous ascendant. The great object which we ought to propose to ourselves is, to acquire a firm and steadfast mind, which the infatuation of passion shall not seduce, nor its violence shake; which resting on fixed principles shall, in the midst of contending emotions, remain free and master of itself; able to listen calmly to the voice of conscience, and prepared to obey its dictates without hesitation.

    To obtain, if possible, such command of passion, is one of the highest attainments of the rational nature. Arguments to show its importance crowd upon us from every quarter. If there be any fertile source of mischief to human life, it is, beyond doubt, the misrule of passion. It is this which poisons the enjoyment of individuals, overturns the order of society, and strews the path of life with so many miseries, as to render it indeed the vale of tears. All those great scenes of public calamity, which we behold with astonishment and horror, have originated from the source of violet passions. These have overspread the earth with bloodshed. These have pointed the assassin's dagger, and filled the poisoned bowl. These, in every age, have furnished too copious materials for the orator's pathetic declamation, and for the poet's tragical song.

    When from public life we descend to private conduct, though passion operates not there in such a wide and destructive sphere, we shall find its influence to be no less baneful. I need not mention the black and fierce passions, such as envy, jealousy, and revenge, whose effects are obviously noxious, and whose agitations are immediate misery. But take any of the licentious and sensual kind. Suppose it to have unlimited scope; trace it throughout its course; and we shall find that gradually, as it rises, it taints the soundness, and troubles the peace of his mind over whom it reigns; that, in its progress, it engages him in pursuits which are marked either with danger or with shame; that, in the end, it wastes his fortune, destroys his health or debases his character; and aggravates all the miseries in which it has involved him, with the concluding pangs of bitter remorse. Through all the stages of this fatal course, how many have heretofore run? What multitudes do we daily behold pursuing it with blind and headlong steps? BLAIR.

SECTION VII.
ON THE PROPER STATE OF OUR TEMPER, WITH RESPECT TO ONE ANOTHER.

    It is evident, in the general, that if we consult

either public welfare or private happiness, Christian charity ought to regulate our disposition in mutual intercourse. But as this great principle admits of several diversified appearances, let us consider some of the chief forms under which it ought to show itself in the usual tenor of life.

What first presents itself to be recommended, is a peaceable temper; a disposition averse to give offence, and desirous of cultivating harmony, and amicable intercourse in society. This supposes yielding and condescending manners, unwillingness to contend with others about trifles, and, in contests that are unavoidable, proper moderation of spirit. Such a temper is the first principle of self enjoyment. It is the basic of all order and happiness among mankind. The positive and contentious, the rude and quarrelsome are the bane of society. They seem destined to blast the small share of comfort which nature has here allotted to man. But they cannot disturb the peace of others, more than they break their own. The hurricane rages first in the own bosom, before it is let forth upon the world. In the tempests which they raise, they are always lost; and frequently it is their lot to perish.

A peaceable temper must be supported by a candid one, or a disposition to view the conduct of others with fairness and impartiality. This stands opposed to a jealous and suspicious temper, which ascribes every action to the worst motive, and throws a black shade over every character. If we would be happy in ourselves, or in our connections with others, let us guard against this malignant spirit. Let us study that charity "which thinketh no evil;" that temper which, without degenerating into credulity, will dispose us to be just; and which can allow us to observe an error, without imputing it as a crime. Thus we shall be kept free from that continual irritation, which imaginary injuries raise in a suspicious breast; and shall walk among men as our brethren not as our enemies.

But to be peaceable, and to be candid is not all that is required of a good man. He must cultivate a kind, generous, and sympathizing temper, which feels for distress, wherever it is beheld; which enters into the concerns of his friends with ardor; and to all with whom he has intercourse, is gently, obliging, and humane. How amiable, appears such a disposition, when contrasted with a malicious or envious temper, which wraps itself up in its own narrow interest, looks with an evil eye on the success of others, and, with an unnatural satisfaction, feeds on their disappointments or miseries! How little does he know of the true happiness of life, who is a stranger to that intercourse of good offices and kind affections, which, by a pleasing charm, attaches men to one another, and circulates joy from heart to heart!

We are not to imagine, that a benevolent temper finds no exercise, unless when opportunities offer of performing actions of high generosity, or of extensive utility. These may seldom occur. The condition of the greater part of mankind in a good measure, precludes them. But in the ordinary round of human affairs, many occasions daily present themselves of mitigating the vexations which others suffer; of soothing their minds; of aiding there interests; of promoting their cheerfulness, or ease. Such occasions may relate to the smaller incidents of life. But let us remember, that of small incidents the system of human life is chiefly composed. The attentions which respect these, when suggested by real benignity of temper, are often more material to the happiness of those around us, than actions which carry the appearance of greater dignity and splendor. No wise or good man ought to account any rules of behaviour as below his regard, which tend to cement the great brotherhood of mankind in comfortable union.

Particularly amidst that familiar intercourse which belongs to domestic life, all the virtues of temper find an ample range. It is very unfortunate, that within that circle men too often think themselves at liberty, to give unrestrained vent to the caprice of passion and humour. Whereas there, on the contrary, more than any where else, it concerns them to attend to the government of their heart; to check what is violent in their tempers, and to soften what is harsh in their manners. For there the temper is formed. There, the real character displays itself. The forms of the world disguise men when abroad. But within his own family, every man is known to be what he truly is. In all our intercourse then with others, particularly in that which is closest and most intimate, let us cultivate a peaceable, a candid, a gentle and friendly temper. This is the temper to which, by repeated injunctions,

our holy religion seeks to form us. This was the temper of Christ. This is the temper of Heaven.
BLAIR.

SECTION VIII.
EXCELLENCE OF THE HOLY SCRIPTURES.

Is it bigotry to believe the sublime truths of the gospel, with full assurance of faith? I glory in such bigotry. I would not part with it for a thousand worlds. I congratulate the man, who is possessed of it: for, amidst all the vicissitudes and calamities of the present state, that man enjoys an inexhaustible fund of consolation, of which it is, not in the power of fortune to deprive him.

There is not a book on earth so favorable to all the kind, and all the sublime affections; or so unfriendly to hatred and persecution, to tyranny, injustice, and every sort of malevolence, as the gospel. It breathes nothing throughout, but mercy, benevolence, and peace.

Poetry is sublime, when it awakens in the mind any great and good affection, as piety, or patriotism. This is one of the noblest effects of the heart. The Psalms are remarkable beyond all other writings, for their power of inspiring devout emotions. But it is not in this respect only, that they are sublime. Of the divine nature, they contain the most magnificent description, that the soul of man can comprehend. The hundred and fourth Psalm, in particular displays the power and goodness of Providence, in creating and preserving the world, and the various tribes of animals in it, with such majestic brevity and beauty, as it is vin to look for in any human composition.

Such of the doctrines of the gospel as are level to human capacity, appear to be agreeable to the purest truth, and the soundest morality. All the genius and learning of the heathen world; all the penetration of Pythagoras, Socrates, and Aristotle, had never been able to produce such a system of moral duty, and so rational an account of Providence and of man, as are to be found in the New Testament. Compared indeed, with this, all other moral and theological wisdom loses, discountenanc'd, and like folly shows. BEATTIE.

SECTION IX.
REFLECTIONS OCCASIONED BY A REVIEW OF THE BLESSINGS, PRONOUNCED BY CHRIST ON HIS DISCIPLES IN HIS SERMON ON THE MOUNT.

What abundant reason have we to thank God, that this large and instructive discourse of our blessed Redeemer, is so particularly recorded by the sacred historian. Let us fix our minds in a posture of humble attention, that we may "receive the law from his mouth."

He opened it with blessings, repeated and most important blessings. But on whom are they pronounced? And whom are we taught to think the happiest of mankind? The meek and the humble; the penitent and the merciful; the peaceful and the pure; those that hunger and thirst after righteousness; those that labour, but faint not, under persecution! Lord! How different are thy maxims from those of the children of this world! They call the proud happy; and admire the gay, the rich, the powerful, and the victorious. But let a vain world take its gaudy trifles and dress up the foolish creatures that pursue them. May our souls share in that happiness which the Son of God came to recommend and to procure! May we obtain mercy of the Lord; may we be owned as his children; enjoy his presence; and inherit his kingdom! With these enjoyments, and these hopes, we will cheerfully welcome the lowest, or the most painful circumstances.

  Let us be animated to cultivate those amiable virtues, which are here recommended to us; this humility and meekness; this penitent sense of sin; this ardent desire after righteousness; this compassion and purity; this peacefulness and fortitude of soul; and, in a word, this universal goodness which becomes us, as we sustain the character of "the salt of the earth," and "the light of the world."

  Is there not reason to lament, that we answer the character no better? Is there not reason to exclaim, with a good man in former times, "Blessed Lord! Either these are not thy words, or we are not Christians!" Oh, season our hearts more effectually with thy grace! Pour forth that divine oil on our lamps! Then shall the flame brighten; then shall the ancient honours of thy religion be revived; and multitudes be awakened and animated by the luster of it, "to glorify our Father in heaven." DODDRIDGE.

Excerpted from
Sermons on Various Subjects, Evangelical, Devotional and Practical, Adapted to the Promotion of Christian Piety, Family Religion, and Youthful Virtue
by Joseph Lathrop, D.D.
Worcester, Massachusetts: Isaiah Thomas, 1793, pp. 44-51

Editor's note: Joseph Lathrop, 1731-1820, was a graduate of Yale College who spent his life as pastor of the Congregational Church in West Springfield, Massachusetts. He was a liberal Calvinist and a fellow of the American Academy of Arts and Sciences.

We of the present generation enjoy the gospel, not for our sakes only, but for the sake of future generations. We are to transmit it to our children, and make such provision for its continuance, that they who come after us may enjoy it as amply as we have done before them. It is committed into our hands, as a sacred deposit, for the benefit of those around us, and those who shall succeed us. While we are working out our own salvation, we are to remember that this is but a part of our work. As it is not solely for our own sakes, that God has given us the means of salvation; so it is not singly on our own account, that we are to value and use them.

The Christian is to attend on the instituted

worship of God, both for his own edification, and for the encouragement of others. He is to live in the practice of all good works, both that he may obtain the reward of righteousness, and that others, beholding his example, may glorify God.

The conversion of a sinner is, in the wisdom and goodness of God, intended for the benefit of others, as well as for the salvation of him, who is the immediate subject of this grace. St. Paul says of himself, "I, who was a blasphemer, a persecutor and injurious, obtained mercy--and the grace of our Lord was exceedingly abundant. Howbeit for this cause I obtained mercy, that in me first Jesus Christ might shew forth all longsuffering for a pattern to them, who should afterward believe on him to life everlasting."

You wonder perhaps why some great sinners are, by the uncommon grace of God, recovered, while others, less guilty than they, are suffered to go on still in their trespasses.

We are not, indeed, very competent judges, who are the greatest sinners, and who have done most to abuse divine grace: But admitting this to be the case, as doubtless it may be, we must remember, that grace is free, and an undeserved benefit conferred on one, is no injury to another. Besides, when great sinners are thus mercifully distinguished, it is not merely for their sakes, but for God's name's sake. As it could not be at all for their worthiness, so neither is it altogether for their benefit; it is also that they may be influential in encouraging the repentance of others.

The conversion of one may be the means or the

occasion of the conversion of many. So it evidently was in the case of Paul. Who could be more injurious to the cause of truth than he was, while he continued a Pharisee? -- Who more useful than he, after he became a Christian? How much evil was prevented--how much good was done, by the conversion of this one man? What an encouragement to sinners under a sense of guilt, is this example of divine mercy? -- How many were converted by Paul's preaching in the course of his ministry? -- What lasting and extensive benefit have mankind received from the writings which he has left? He was a chosen vessel to Christ to bear his name among the Gentiles, as well as the Jews. His natural abilities, his education and accomplishments, when his heart was sanctified by grace, eminently qualified him for so great a work.

The conversion of every sinner has its uses, within a narrower sphere. Every convert is bound to improve, for the benefit of others, the grace of God toward him. "When thou are converted, strengthen thy brethren;" is Christ's command to Peter. This was David's prayer and resolution, "Create in me a clean heart--uphold me with thy free spirit; then will I teach transgressors thy ways, and sinners shall be converted unto thee."

I proceed to observe,

II. As *personal* blessings are designed for the benefit of many, so blessings granted to *societies* are intended for the general good of mankind.

The national deliverance of the Jews from the Egyptian servitude, and afterward from the

Babylonian captivity, was vouchsafed, not so much to render *them* important, as to display the glory of God's name among the heathen. The publick institutions of religion enjoyed by them, were made subservient to the happiness of many other nations.

Revolutions in favour of liberty, in a particular country, may be productive of interesting consequences in lands far remote, and in ages long to come.

The revolution, which has taken place in America, is operating to great, and we hope, happy events elsewhere. What God has done for us, was not only for our sakes, but for the benefit of mankind in other regions of the globe, and in other periods of time. And though Liberty in her progress, will meet with violent opposition, and, in her conflicts, will suffer dire calamities, yet we cannot doubt, but she will finally triumph.

We trust also, that this revolution will prove friendly to the interest of pure religion.

It is indeed complained, that infidelity much prevails. But perhaps its prevalence is more in appearance, than in reality; and it rather throws off its former disguise, than gains additional strength. There is greater freedom of inquiry, and more liberality of sentiment, than in years past: Learning is also more cultivated, and knowledge more generally diffused. That spirit of liberty, which sprang up here, and is now spreading in the world, will probably render the civil governments of nations more tolerant to free religion, as well as more congenial to the rights of mankind. As learning becomes more common in the body of the people, it will of course be deemed a more requisite qualification in the publick teachers of religion; and ignorant pretenders, and designing impostors, will be more easily discerned, and more effectually discountenanced. As the light of truth beams on mankind, superstition and enthusiasm will retire to their primeval darkness; and rational, substantial religion will stand for confessed in all its divine beauties. The truth will bear the strictest inquiry. And though, in an inquisitive age, some novel opinions may be started and pursued for a while, yet truth will eventually be more extensively known, and more firmly believed.

The changes, which we have seen, probably will never answer all the purposes, which worldly wisdom has contemplated; but they will answer the greater and better purposes of divine wisdom. They have already contributed much, and doubtless will contribute more to the advancement of useful knowledge, liberality of sentiment, and the intercourse of nations: And as these are advanced, there will be more room for religion to have free course and be glorified.

We are apt to contemplate events on the partial scale of self interest. The Deity views them on the extended scale of benevolence. Our selfish expectations are usually disappointed. The purposes of divine goodness will be accomplished. If we regard events only in reference to our private interests, we shall never find them agreeable to our wishes. But if we believe that the divine government is good, and will extend to all nations and ages, looks forward to the most distant connexions of things, and moves the whole chain of events, then we may acquiesce in its dispensations, however unfavorable to our private views. Benevolence will rejoice in the belief of God's general goodness, when selfishness murmurs at the disappointment of its own groveling designs.

Farther--The gospel, which is given to a particular people, is given them for the benefit of other nations--not merely for their own.

The Apostle observes, that the preaching and reception of it in Thessalonica, proved the means of its general diffusion; for from thence sounded out the word of God, through Macedonia and Achaia; yea, in every place the faith of the Thessalonians was spread abroad. He says to the Ephesians, "God who is rich in mercy--hath quickened us together with Christ, that in the ages to come, he might shew forth the exceeding riches of his grace in

his kindness to us by Jesus Christ." "He had made known unto us the mystery of his will, according to the good pleasure which he purposed in himself, that in the dispensation of the fulness of times, he might gather together in one all things in Christ, both which are in heaven, and which are in earth...." How unsearchable are his judgments, and his ways past finding out! But,

III. We may rise still higher in our contemplation of this wonderful connexion of God's works.

As favours to particular persons may be publick blessings; and national blessings may extend their influence to mankind in general; so God's mercies to the human race may operate to the benefit of other intelligences; as the sun beams, which enlighten the earth, are reflected back to the skies.

When God sent his Son from heaven to redeem us from guilt and ruin, it was not for our sakes only, but for his name's sake, that the glory of his wisdom, grace and holiness might be displayed throughout the whole intellectual world. The angels in heaven praise God for the wonders of his redeeming love to mankind. They give glory to him, that there is in earth peace, good will to men. They desire to look into this astonishing scheme, which, by the publication of the gospel is opened to *their* view, as well as *ours*. Paul was sent to preach among the Gentiles the unsearchable riches of Christ, not only to make *men* see what is the fellowship of the mystery, which had been hidden from ages; but also to the intent, that *now unto principalities and powers in heavenly places* might be known by the church the manifold wisdom of God. Angels now join with saints in the new song to him who was slain, and has redeemed us by his blood: And every intellectual and virtuous being, through the creation of, ascribes, and will ascribe, riches and blessing, and glory and honour to him who sits on the throne, and to the Lamb forever and ever.

Sermon VII.
The Nature of Religious Truths
by Samuel Clarke, D.D.
Excerpted from Sermons by Samuel Clarke published from the Author's Manuscript, by John Clarke, DD.
Dean of Sarum
London: W. Botham, 1730, Vol. III, pp. 145-166

Editor's Note: Dr. Samuel Clarke, 1675-1729, was Rector of St. James, Westminster.

2 Tim. 2:25.
In Meekness instructing those that oppose themselves, if God peradventure will give them Repentance to the acknowledging of the Truth.

As *Light* is necessarily and essentially different from *darkness*, notwithstanding those who are blind cannot distinguish That difference; so, notwithstanding the Weakness and Blindness of mens Understandings, and the much worse Confusion arising from the Corruption and Perverseness of their Wills; yet *Truth* is still in the nature of things, always real and invariable, and for the most part, *distinguishable* also from *Error*. In some kinds of things, 'tis indeed very difficult for us to discover where the truth lies; the causes of things, being abstruse; the ends and designs of them, remote; the things themselves, often intricate; the manner how they may possibly be, diverse and various; and our understanding, in itself finite and fallible. But tis difficulty of finding out the truth, is generally in things of that nature only; which are of no great importance for us to know. As the eyes of our body, are fitted only to discern things within the reach of such a distance, as 'tis of use to us in life to comprehend within our view; so our understanding, which is the eye of the mind, can very difficultly search into the truth of numberless things which it does not concern us distinctly to know. But in all things of importance, in all things of great and real use to us, such as are the eternal differences of good and evil, and all matters fundamental in religion; in these things, truth is always as distinguishable to the unprejudiced understanding of a person even of a mean capacity, as light is by the eye distinguishable from dankness.

That God, the maker and judge of all, is to be worshipped, rather than the fictions of human folly. That the worship most acceptable to him, is the obedience of a virtuous and sober life, rather than an endless circle of mere external ceremonies. That the practice of justice, righteousness, meekness and charity, is much more useful to men, than their stirring up each others zeal for or against opinions, of which they understand very little: These great lines of truth, are so plainly, so brightly conspicuous, both in reason and scripture, that *he who runs may read them.* Whosoever is led into any error, contrary to these *great and fundamental truths,* 'tis not by his understanding, but by his will that he is deceived; and therefore he is justly answerable for his foly. *God would have all men to be saved, and to come to the knowledge of the truth,* I Tim. 2:4. The light held forth to them is clear and strong; the rules are few and conspicuous; that an unprejudiced person would hardly think it possible they should be mistaken. Yet so extensive is that kind of error which proceeds from the willfulness and corrupt affections, that in opposition to these great and plain rules it is, that the *whole world lieth in wickedness,* I John 5:19. In opposition to the evidence of this shining light it is, that the d3evotion of the *popish* world is transferred from the God and Father of all things, and from the one only Mediator whom *He* has appointed; to saints, and angels, and images, and fictitious relicks. In opposition to the same plain and evident truths it is, that, not in the popish world only, but in too great a part even of that also which calls itself *Protestant,* mere outward and customary forms have by many persons a great stress laid upon them, than the weightier matters of the law, practice of true virtue: and men generally are more concerned to support uncertain opinions, than to promote the habits of justice, goodness, temperance, meekness, and universal good-will towards mankind; upon which principally depends our happiness in this world, and our title to that which is to come. This is the great corruption, the great and universal error of all ages in matters of religion. And they who thus *oppose themselves* to the great end and design of the gospel, subverting the simplicity and purity of the doctrine of

Christ; these, as well as the atheistically, debauched, and profane, are the persons whom we ought to be continually *instructing in meekness, if God peradventure will give them repentance to the acknowledgment of the truth.*

    In which words of the Apostle, we may observe distinctly the following particulars. 1st, A supposition laid down; that truth is something real in itself, and of importance to Men; something that may be found, and which we ought to seek after. 2dly, An observation made concerning the corrupt state and disposition of mankind; that some there will always be, who will set themselves to oppose the truth. 3dly, A direction given, concerning our own duty; that we ought to instruct such persons, in meekness. And 4thly, a reason added, why we ought to do it in that manner; if God peradventure will give them repentance to the acknowledgment of the truth.

    1st. Here is a supposition laid down; that truth, is something real itself, and of importance to men; something that may be found, and which we ought to seek after. I have already observed, that where-ever the Scripture speaks of truth, it always means such truth as has relation to religion; and I shall use the word in that sense, thro' the whole following discourse. *All* truth, of what kind soever it be, is real; but not always of importance. *All* truth, has its *foundation in nature*; but is not always necessary, or of any great use for us to know. But truth in matters of religion, is always of the greatest importance; as being the foundation and the support, of right practice.

Men, upon erroneous principles, may do what is right by chance; or the general probity of their temper, may overrule the ill influence of mistake principles: But there can be no certain, there can be no steady rule of good practice, without a Foundation of truth. All error is founded in imagination only; 'tis a shadow, without a substance; 'tis generally nothing else, but a careless following of other mens opinions, or pretended opinions; a lazy and formal adherence to the customs of the age men live in, or the notions which happen to prevail, like other fashions, in particular places, and among certain sects or parties of men. Principles of which kind, can be no better a foundation of practice, than mere chance; and religion built upon such a quick-sand, is, in the several nations of the earth, nothing at all more than the custom or fashion of the country. Religion acceptable to God, who judges the heart; must be, in the mind of every particular person, a love of truth and right: A love of that truth and right, not which is esteemed such upon mere vulgar and customary acceptation, but which the mind itself perceives and feels, and, upon examination finds to be so in reality. Of this, the mind of every uncorrupt man, is by the author of nature made as competent a judge; as the eyes of the body, are made fit to discern between light and darkness. And the righteousness of God's future judgment, (*that judgment* wherein men shall give an account of themselves, not in the lump by sects and parties, but every man singly and personally for himself; the righteousness, I say, of *that future judgment)* must of necessity depend, upon every man's understanding for himself the rule he is to be judged by. What this rule is, can be of no difficulty for any man to discover. *Natural conscience, that original light, that candle of the Lord,* which God has implanted in every man's breast, tells him always what it is, with regard to the eternal truths of morality: And to them who live under the light of the Gospel, the additional precepts given by Christ in scripture, are no less clear and conspicuous. These truths of God, are, like an immovable rock, the basis and foundation of that true religion, which approves itself to every man's understanding by clear reason, and glorifies God by making men like unto him through virtue and righteousness in their practice. All false religions consist, in changing these truths of God into a lie, Rom. 1:25. Either corrupting the Truth of God's creation, by introducing into religion things opposite to, or things which draw men from, the practice of virtue, of justice, goodness and charity. Or corrupting the truth of God's revelation, by mixing with the plain simplicity of the doctrine of Christ, traditions and uncertain notions of merely humane invention. Truth itself, both *natural* and *revealed*, when separate from all corruptions of men, appears always with a native luster and beauty, with a strength and clearness of reason, which the scripture elegantly compares to a light shining in darkness; which needs no external force, no violence or compulsion, no artificial imposing upon the understanding, (as the inventions of men do,) to cause it to be received and embraced;

but it requires only an *unprejudiced apprehension,* and an *uncorrupt will,* in order to its being entertained universally in the love thereof. It always tends also to promote mens *true interest*; their true interest, as well temporal as eternal: The Peace and satisfaction, of every man's own mind in particular; and, in general, universal love and good-will towards all others. For all the contentions and animosities, all the hatred and malice, all the persecution and cruelties which have ever been exercised in the world under pretense of zeal for religion; have in reality always arisen purely upon account of zeal for matters of mens own invention, never out of concern for the plain laws and commands of God. And all the dark and slavish bigotry, which has at any time tormented the minds of particular men; has been owing to the superstitious errors, wherewith the weakness of some, and the designs of others, have misrepresented the truth of God, which the Apostle stiles *the perfect law of liberty*; and of which, our Savior himself declares, John 8:32, *Ye shall know the truth, and the truth shall make you free.* Not without the greatest reason therefore, is that exhortation of the wise man, Prov. 23:23, *Buy the truth, and sell it not:* And 4:7, *Wisdom is the principal thing; therefore get wisdom; and with all thy getting, get understanding.* St Paul in like manner, Phil. 4:8, in that elegant enumeration, wherein he reckons up every thing that can be thought to be excellent; and exhorts the Philippians, in the most earnest and affectionate manner, *If there be any virtue, if there be an praise,* to *think upon* those things; not without a particular emphasis, placeth at the head of all, in the very first rank, *whatsoever things are true.* And this may suffice, for explication of the first particular in the text; the supposition laid down, that truth is something real in itself, and of importance to men; something that may be found, and which we ought to seek after.

2dly. The next observation collected from the words of the text, is; that such is the corrupt state and disposition of mankind, that *some* there will *always be*, who will set themselves to oppose the truth. Notwithstanding the strength and clearness of reason, with which it is generally accompanied; notwithstanding the apparent benefit and advantage, which the knowledge of truth always brings to mankind; yet so little sensible are men of the intrinsic excellency of things, so inattentive to the strength of the clearest reason, so apt to be imposed upon in judging concerning their own true interest; that nothing is more common, than to see the plainest and most useful truths, in matters of religion, violently and passionately opposed.

The principal causes of this opposition; are in particular, ignorance, carelessness, prejudice, and vice.

The first cause of men's setting themselves in opposition to the light of truth, is ignorance. Meaning here, by ignorance, not a bare want of knowledge: (For the natural and proper effect of bare want of knowledge, is, that men forbear to pass any judgement at all, upon what they understand not; and that they neither contend for nor against any opinion, before they have some reason to determine them so to do: But there is a presumptuous ignorance, which despises knowledge; and this makes men oppose the truth, before they understand any thing of it. Seest thou a man that despiseeth instruction? There is more hope of a fool, than of him.

ANOTHER cause of men's opposing truth, is carelessness. They blindly, and without any consideration, follow the customs of the place where they happen to live; and the knowledge of truth, seems to them to be of no great importance. They take up their religion at adventures, not from the consideration of the laws of nature or of revelation, but merely from the company they chance to be educated amongst; and thus all religions are put upon an equal foot, varying according to the accidental temper of the persons among whom they prevail. Men of this disposition, careless of finding out the truth, and consequently having indeed no religion at all, but barely the name and profession of it; generally prefer any degree of ignorance, before the carefullest study either of the nature of things, or of the laws of God. To this temper 'tis palpably owing, that so many whole nations at this day, pagans and Mohometans, never give themselves the trouble to enquire at all, whether the Christian religion be true or no; and even among the professors of Christianity, (as they think themselves to be,) many entire nations, full of men very learned and of great abilities, yet never suffer any careful inquiry to be made, whether the worship of imaginary saints, and of images of wood and stone, and of relicks, and of bread; and innumerable other doctrines and practices, absurd notions and superstitious ceremonies; they never (I say) suffer any careful examination to be made, whether these things are agreeable to the plainness and simplicity, to the holiness and purity of Christ's religion, or no.

    A further cause of men's opposing the truth, is prejudice. They are not perhaps naturally ignorant; nor yet of so lazy and careless a temper as to oppose the truth merely to avoid the trouble of studying it. But their prejudices are so strong, that the clearest light cannot overcome and dissipate so thick a cloud. They have accustomed themselves to found their belief entirely in an implicit reliance upon other men; instead of building it upon the evidence of things themselves, which is the foundation of truth. And then, the traditions of the scribes and elders and Pharisees; the decrees of popes, or the determinations of parties, evidently governed by worldly motives; shall have much more weight with them, to perswade them to blind or shut their eyes; than the whole scripture of truth, or the strongest and plainest reason in the world, shall have to perswade them to open them. So little do they consider those admonitions of our Saviour; *Search the scriptures;* and, *He that hath ears to hear, let him hear*: And that of St Paul; *I speak as unto wise men,* (that is, to intelligent persons;) *judge ye what I say,* I Cor. 10:15. And of St Peter, I Pet. 3:15. *Be ready always to give an answer to every man that asketh you a reason of the hope that is in you.*

But the last and greatest reason of men's setting themselves in opposition to the truth, is the wickedness and corruption of their manners; the love of unrighteousness and debauchery, the desire of power and dominion, the concern they are under for the defense and support of a sect or party, without having any knowledge how far they are, or are not, in the right. These are things, which make men to shut their eyes against the light, to love and choose darkness rather than light, and wilfully to stop their ears against all the means of being better informed. Concerning such persons, St Paul prophecies, 2 Tim 3:2, 5, 8. *In the last days....men shall be....boasters,....despisers of those that are good, ...heady, high-minded, lovers of pleasures more than lovers of god, having a form of godliness, but denying the power thereof, ...resisting the truth, men of corrupt minds.* And these things must be, saith the same Apostle; (I.e. 'tis fit and just that the Providence of God should permit it thus to be;) *that those which are approved,* (I.e. that those who seek and obey the truth and simplicity of the gospel, separate from all worldly and unjustifiable designs,) *may be made manifest among you.*

3dly. The third thing observable in the text, is the direction given us concerning our own duty; that we ought in meekness to instruct those who oppose themselves against the truth. He who himself, suffers for well-doing, and for the testimony of a good conscience, is sure of being (at least *so far*) in the right: But he who does violence to others; if they, whom he does violence to, be in a right cause, he is an enemy to God: But if they be in the wrong, yet he dishonours the truth, by acting unrighteous for it, and not knowing what Spirit he is of. *The servant of the Lord, must not strive, but be gentle unto all men, apt to teach, patient.* We cannot always discern, who they are that error thro' ignorance, and who thro' a vitious disposition. (I speak not here concerning matters of immorality; for faults of this kind, are evident to all men.) But if we would, yet meekness is at all times necessarily a *fruit of the spirit*; and we are commanded to be patient towards all men, I Th. 5:14, towards them that oppose, as well as towards them that are only ignorant of, the truth. *Who is the wise man,* saith St James, *and indued with knowledge amongst you? let him show out of a good conversation his works with meekness of wisdom.* For----*the wisdom that is from above, is first pure, then peaceable, gentle and easy to be intreated.* But, *anger, resteth in the bosom of fools,* Eccles. 7:9. And the *wrath of man, worketh not the righteousness of God,* James 1:20. Being always a certain evidence, that men are more concerned for some temporal interest, than for the real honour of God and goodness. Men of a true Christian spirit, sincerely desirous to promote the knowledge of truth and the practice of virtue in the world, rather than the obtaining of temporal power and dominion for themselves are always willing to consider, that they themselves are fallible; and therefore constantly endeavour to convince others by the methods of reason, and not of passion and violence. *Shewing all meekness unto all men, for* that *we ourselves also were sometimes foolish,* Tit 3:2-3. Which temper, is much more reasonable in point of truth and error; when, even with regard to faults of the will, St Paul admonishes, *if a man be overtaken in a fault,----restore such a one in the spirit of meekness, considering thyself, lest thou also be tempted,* Gal. 6:1. (He speaks not of the crimes of malefactors, such as must necessarily be punished by the had of justice; but he means such faults, as are to be cured by reproof.) *Our Saviour himself,* tho' infallible, and could *not* err; *yet was meek and lowly in Heart:* And rebuked his disciples with great severity, when once upon high provocation they discovered an inclination to violent methods; *Ye know not* (said he) *what manner of spirit ye are of,* Luke 9:55. Plainly intimating to all succeeding generations , wherein would like the principal difference between the *Spirit of Christ* and the *Spirit of Anti-Christ.*

  4*thly* and lastly; HERE is in the text annexed a particular reason, with regard to the persons to be instructed; why our instruction to them, ought always to be accompanied with meekness…. We are to instruct them with meekness; least peradventure, by our heat and passion, we raise in them a just prejudice against us; when, by meek instruction, they might possibly have been brought to repentance, and to the acknowledgment of the truth: And so we, by our ill behaviour, become answerable for their miscarriage. For, nothing can be a greater hindrance to men's being convinced, than the applying violence and pssion instead of reason: And nothing can give more advantage to the evidence of truth, than the meek behaviour of those who profess it. For this reason, we so frequently find repeated in scripture the following admonitions, which may serve for a proper application of this whole discourse. *Be ready always to give an answer to every man that asketh you a reason of the hope that is in you, with* meekness *and fear,* I Pet. 3:15. *Give none offense, neither to the Jews, nor to the Gentiles,* I Cor. 10:32. *Walk in wisdom towards them that are without,* Col. 4:5. *Have a good report of them which art without, lest ye fall into reproach,* I Tim. 3:7. *Let your Moderation,* your meek and exemplary good Spirit, *be known unto all men,* Phil. 4:5. *Blameless and harmless, the sons of God, without rebuke, in the midst of a crooked and perverse generation, among whom ye shine as lights in the world,* Phil. 2:15. *Having your conversation honest,* that is, of good reputation, even *among the Gentiles; that whereas they speak against you as evil-doers, they may by your good works which they shall behold, glorify God in the day of visitation,* I Pet. 2:12. And in the words of our Saviour himself, Matt. 5:16. *Let your light so shine before men;* the light of your meekness, goodness and charity; the light of your excellent temper, and universal virtue; that the whole world *may see your good works, and glorify your father which is in heaven.*

Excerpted from
Grigg & Elliot's New Series of Common School Readers,
The Pleasing Companion; or Second Reader
Section XVII. *Gray Hairs made Happy.*
Edited by Jesse Torrey, Jun.
Philadelphia: Grigg & Elliot, 1845

Editor's note: Jesse Torrey, Jun., 1787-1834, was an American physician, an early advocate of the abolition of slavery, and a champion of the "the universal dissemination of knowledge and virtue by means of free public libraries."

1. OPPOSITE to the house in which Juliet's parents lived, was a little opening, ornamented with a grass-plot, and overshaded by a venerable tree, commanding an extensive view before it. On this delightful spot, Juliet used frequently to sit in her little chair, while employed in knitting stockings for her mother.

2. As she was one day thus employed, she saw a poor old man advancing very slowly towards her. His hair was as white as silver, and his back bent with age; he supported himself by a stick, and seemed to walk with great difficulty. "Poor man, said Juliet, looking at him most tenderly, he seems to be very much in paid, and perhaps is very poor, which are two dreadful evils!"

3. She also saw a number of boys who were

following close behind this poor old man. They passed jokes upon this threadbare coat, which had very long skirts and short sleeves, contrary to the fashion of those days. His hat, which was quite rusty, did not escape their notice; his cheeks were hollow and his body thin.

4. These wicked boys no sooner saw him, than they all burst out laughing. A stone lay in his way, which he did not perceive, and over it he stumbled, and had like to have fallen. This afforded them sport, and they laughed loudly; but it gave great paid to the old man, who uttered a deep sigh.

5. "I once was as young as you are, said he to the boys, but I did not laugh at the infirmities of age as you do. The day will come in which you will be old yourselves, and every day is bringing you nearer to that period. You will then be sensible of the impropriety of your present conduct."

6. Having thus spoken, he endeavoured to hobble on again, and made a second stumble, when, in struggling to save himself from falling, he dropped his cane, and down he fell. On this the wicked boys renewed their laugh, and highly enjoyed his misfortune.

7. Juliet, who had seen every thing that had passed, could not help pitying the old man's situation, and therefore putting down her stocking on the chair, she ran towards him, picked up the cane and gave it him, and then taking hold of his other arm, as if she had been as strong as a woman, advised him to lean upon her, and not mind any thing the boys might say

to him.

8. The poor old man looking at her very earnestly, "Sweet child," said he, "how good you are! this kindness makes me, in a moment, forget all the ill behaviour of those naughty boys. May you ever be happy." They then walked on together; but the boys being probably made ashamed of their conduct by the behaviour of Juliet, followed the old man no further.

9. While the boys were turning about, one of them fell down also, and all the rest began laughing as they had before done at the old man. He was very angry with them on that account, and as soon as he got up ran after his companions, pelting them with stones.

10. He instantly became convinced, how unjust it was to laugh at the distresses of another, and formed a resolution for the future, never to laugh at any person's paid. He followed the old man he had been laughing at, though at some distance, wishing for an opportunity to do him some favour, by way of atonement, for what he had done.

11. The good old man, in the mean time, by the kind assistance of Juliet, proceeded with slow but sure steps. She asked him to stop and rest himself a little, and told him that her house was that before him. "Pray stay," said she, "and sit a little under that large tree. My parents, indeed, are not at home, and therefore you will not be quite so well treated; yet it will be a little rest to you."

12. The old man accepted Juliet's offer. She brought him out a chair, and then fetched some bread

and cheese, and good small beer, which were all the pretty maid could get at. He thanked her very kindly, and then entered into conversation with her. "I find, my dear, said he, "you have parents. I doubt not but you love them, and they love you. They must be very happy, and may they always continue to be so!"

13. "And pray, good old man," said Juliet, "I doubt not but you have children." -- "I had a son, replied he, who lived in Albany, loved me tenderly, and frequently came to see me; but alas! He is now dead, and I am left disconsolate. His widow indeed is rich; but she assumes the character of the lady, and thinks it beneath her to inquire whether I am dead or living, as she does not wish it to be known that her husband's father is a poor man."

14. Juliet was much affected, and could hardly believe that such cruel people existed. "Ah! certain I am, said she, that my dear mother would not behave so cruel." He then rose and thanked Juliet with a blessing; but she was determined not to leave him, till she had accompanied him a little further.

15. As they walked on, they saw the little boy who had been following them; for he ran on some way before, and was then sitting on the grass: When they looked upon him he cast his eyes downwards, got up after they had passed, and followed them again. Juliet observed him, but said nothing.

16. She asked the old man if he lived alone. "No, little lady, answered he, I have a cottage on the other side of the meadow, seated in the middle of a little garden, with an orchard and a small field. An

old neighbour whose cottage fell down through age, lives with me and cultivates my ground.

17. "He is an honest man, and I am perfectly easy in his society; but the loss of my son still bears hard upon me, nor have I the happiness to see any of his children, who must by this time have forgotten me."

18. These complaints touched the heart of Juliet, who told him, that she and her mother would come and see him. The sensibility and kindness of this little girl served only to aggravate his grief, by bringing to his mind the loss he had sustained in his son. Tears came in his eyes when he pulled out his handkerchief to wipe them; and, instead of again putting it into his pocket, in the agitation of his mind, it slipped aside, and fell unnoticed by him or Juliet.

19. The little boy who followed them, saw the handkerchief fall, ran to pick it up and gave it the old man, saying, "Here good old man, you dropped your handkerchief, and here it is." -- "Thank you heartily my little friend said the old man. Here is a good natured lad, who does not ridicule ole age nor laugh at the afflictions that attend it. You will certainly become an honest man. Come both of you to my habitation, and I will give you some milk."

20. They had no sooner reached the old man's cottage than he brought out some milk, and the best bread he had, which though coarse, was good. They all sat down upon the grass, and made a comfortable repast. However, Juliet began to be afraid her parents might come home, and be uneasy at her absence; and

the little boy was sorry to go, but was sadly afraid, should he stay, of being scolded by his mother.

BERQUIN.

21.   --------To bless is to be blest!
We led the bending beggar on his way;
(Bare were his feet, his tresses silver gray)
Sooth'd the keen pangs his aged spirit felt,
And on his tale with more attention dwelt.
As in his script we dropt our little store,
And wept to think that little was no more,
He breath'd his pray'r, "Long may such goodness live!"
'Twas all he gave, 'twas all he had to give.

Excerpted from
Chapter XXXVIII "On the Education of Children",
pp. 241-242 of

The Complete Duty of Man: Or, A System of Doctrinal and Practical Christianity

By H. Venn, Rector of Yelling, and Chaplain to the Earl of Buchan
Worcester: Printed by Sewall Goodridge, 1804, First American Edition

Editor's note: Henry Venn, 1725-1797, was an English evangelical Anglican minister.

...it is a duty all parents owe their children to inure them to *industry*, to inspire them with a contempt and abhorrence of idleness, as the great corrupter of the human mind and inlet to every vice. The poor must strongly insist upon their children's giving themselves diligently to work, not only as necessary to get their bread, but as the only means of keeping them from pilfering and theft, from infamy and the gallows. The children of the rich stand in no less need of being excited to industrious application of their time and talents. From their earliest years they should hear, it is not wealth, a large estate, or even nobility of birth which can preserve them from being truly despicable and malignant to mankind, unless they *take pains* to acquire what will improve the mind, and give them ability to perform the duty they owe society; that without love of employment suited to their high station, they, like truant school-boys, must seek men as idle as themselves for company; and to kill time, must be eager in the chase after foolish amusements, not above the size of a little school-boy's mind; and even sink into all meanness and the horrid wickedness of a debauched life, to find in that sink, their chief pleasure. On the contrary, by love of study and fine writes, by being active and useful, by cultivating their advantages in station, they will never feel time a burden on their hands. They will be independent on a thousand trifles, which agitate and vex their equals. They will always be doing good, and be honorable in their generation. These instructions, enforced by the very conduct they inculcate, will work mightily as an antidote to the intoxicating pride, which wealth and grandeur naturally inspire. They will readily then believe they were not born only to please themselves. Conduct, I observe, must enforce these precepts, for if the persons who give them, violate them too, they can have not effect, because children must necessarily believe their parents judge that to be the way of pleasure and happiness in which they see them walk, because they do so out of choice; and if they did not think it best, why should they choose it? As it will, therefore, appear cruel in parents to correct or reprove for tempers and practices their children learn from themselves, so it will be absurd to expect precept or reproof should profit them, when the persons from whom they come, are not under their influence.

After the welfare of the soul, and the improvement of the min have been duly consulted, one attention more is necessary in parents, viz. to make provision for their children, sufficient, if they can, to enable them by honest industry, or some liberal profession, to support themselves, and be useful members of society. For what can be more contrary to the feelings of parental love, than by idleness or extravagance to expose their offspring to poverty, or to force them to settle in a station of life much beneath that in which they were born, a cause frequently of much vexation to them, and a bitter disappointment which few are able to bear. But with regard to what may properly be called a provision, reason not fashion, the word of God, not blind affection, must determine. When persons who were born to no estate, amass wealth with a design to raise their children above the want of any employment or profession, scanty must be their charities, and strong their love of money. Yet so far is opulence from being any real benefit to children that (few instances excepted) it proves a corrupter of their hearts a pander to their lusts, fixing them in habits of vanity, extravagance, and luxury.

The last duty I shall mention, which parents owe to their children, is to pray to God for them; for though the methods of religious instruction mentioned, have a natural tendency to do much good, they cannot of themselves convert the heart to God. You may take all pains for this purpose, but still those who receive the *Lord Jesus Christ*, are born not of blood, nor of flesh, nor of the will of man, but of God. Therefore you must humbly and earnestly pray to him for success in your attempts, that as the inhabitants of the world are increased by your offspring, an addition may be made by their names to the church of the living God, and the inhabitants of heaven.

Excerpted from Sermon II
"The Unreasonableness of Indetermination in Religion", pp. 41-46
in

Twenty Sermons, on Various Subjects
(From an Edinburgh Edition.)
by Jonathan Edwards
Carlisle: Printed by George Kline, 1803

Editor's note: Jonathan Edwards, 1703-1758, is widely regarded as America's most important philosophical theologian. His preaching helped shape "The First Great Awakening" that swept the American colonies in the 1730's and 1740's leaving a permanent impact on American Religion. In later years her served briefly as president of the College of New Jersey until his death caused by a smallpox inoculation.

I Kings 18:21
And Elijah came unto all the people, and said, How long halt ye between two opinions? If the Lord be God, follow him; but if Baal, then follow him. And the people answered him not a word.

....

APPLICATION.

I. Let this put every one upon *examining* himself, whether or no he have ever yet come to a full determination in the affair of religion.

First, Inquire whether or no you have ever yet come to a full determination with respect to the *truth* of the things of religion. Have you ever been fully convinced? Is it a question which has been answered and determined with you, whether there be a future state; or does it yet remain a question with you unresolved? Are you not yet to seek whether there be any future state, and whether or no the story about Jesus Christ be any more than a fable? Here I desire you to note two things.

 1. If the main reason why you assent to the truth of religion be, that others believe so, and you have been so instructed from your childhood; you are of those with whom the truth of religion yet remains undetermined. Tradition and education will never fix and settle the mind in a satisfactory and effectual belief of the truth of religion. Though men, taking religion upon trust, may seem to give a full assent to the truth of religion, and not to call it in question; yet such a faith will not stand a shock; a temptation easily overthrows it: The reason of man in time of trial will not rest on so poor evidence as that.

 There are multitudes who seem to grant the truth of religion, with whom the main foundation of their faith is the tradition of their fathers, or the profession of their neighbours; and it is to be feared, it is so with many who count themselves good Christians. But as to all such persons as never have seen any other evidence to satisfy them, either of the truth or falsehood of religion, they are they that halt between two opinions.--The same may be said of those who are unstable in their *disposition* with regard to Christ or the things which he taught.

 2. If you are fully come to a determination

concerning the things of religion, that they are true, they will be of weight with you above all things in the world. If you be really convinced that these things are true, that they are no fable, but reality, it is impossible but that you must be influenced by them above all things in the world; for these things are so great, and so infinitely exceed all temporal things, that it cannot be otherwise. He that really is convinced that there is a heaven and hell, and an eternal judgement; that the soul, as soon as parted from the body, appears before the judgment-seat of God; and that the happiness and misery of a future state is as great as the Scripture represents it; or that Gold is as holy, just, and jealous, as he hath declared concerning himself in his word; I say, he that is really convinced and hath settled it with himself that these things are certainly true; will regard them and be influenced by them above all things in the world. He will be more concerned by far how he shall escape eternal damnation, and have the favour of God and eternal life, than how he shall get the world, gratify the flesh, please his neighbours, get honour, or obtain any temporal advantage whatsoever. His main inquiry will not be, what shall I eat, and what shall I drink, &c. but he will seek first the kingdom of God and his righteousness.

Examine yourselves therefore by this: Are not your hearts chiefly set upon the world and the things of it? Is it not more your concern, care, and endeavour to further your outward interests, than to secure an interest in heaven? And is not this the very reason that you have never seen the reality of eternal things.

Secondly, Inquire whether you have ever yet come to a determination about religion with respect to the practice of it; whether you have chosen heaven with the way to it, viz. the way of obedience and self-denial, before this world and the ways of sin; whether you have determined upon it as most eligible, to devote yourselves to the service of God.--Here I shall mention three or four things which are signs that men halt between two opinions in this matter.

1. To put off duty till hereafter.--When persons love to keep their duty at a distance, engage not in it for the present, but chuse to keep at a little distance from it; when they think of engaging in religion in better earnest in a little time, when they shall so and so be under better conveniencies for it, but do it not now, do not make haste without delay; when they are very good *intenders* concerning what they will do to-morrow, but very poor *performers* to-day; when they say, as Felix, "go thy way for this time, when I have a convenient season I will call for thee;" when these things are so, it is a sign that they halt between two opinions, and have never as yet come to a full determination with respect to the practice of religion.--Those that have once fully determined that religion is necessary and eligible, will not desire to put it off, but will make it their present and immediate business.

2. It is a sign of the same thing when persons are strict and conscientious in some things, but not in all, not universal in their obedience; do some duties, but live in the omission of others; avoid some sins,

but allow themselves in others; are conscientious with respect to the duties of worship public and private, but not in their behaviour to their neighbours; are not just in their dealings, nor conscientious in paying their debts; nor do to others as they would that they should do to them; but have crooked perverse ways in their dealings among mankind.

    The same may be said when they are just in their dealings and trade with men, but are not conscientious in other things; indulge sensual appetites, drink to excess, or allow themselves in wanton practices: Or are honest and temperate, but licentious in using their tongues, backbiting and reproaching their fellow men, 2 Tim. 3:6-7.

    3. It is a sign that you halt between two opinions, if you sometimes are wont to be considerably engaged in religion, but at other times neglect it; sometimes forming a resolution to be in good earnest, then dropping it again; sometimes seeming to be really engaged in seeking salvation, and very earnest in religious duties; at other times wholly taken up about the things of the world, while religion is neglected, and religious duties are omitted.

    These things shows that you are yet unsettled, have never yet come to a full determination concerning religion, but are halting between two opinions, and therefore are thus unstable in all your ways, and proceed thus by fits and starts in religion, James 1:6-8. "But let him ask in faith, nothing wavering: for he that wavereth is like a wave of the sea, driven with the wind and tossed. For let not that man think that he shall receive any thing of the Lord. A double-minded man is unstable in all his ways." If your determination were fixed in religion, you would be more steady in your practice.

 4. It is a sign that you are halting between two opinions, if it be your manner to balk your duty whenever any notable difficulty comes in the way, considerably cross to your interest, or very inconsistent with your ease or convenience, or your temporal honour. Whatever zeal you may seem to have, whatever concern about the things of religion, and however strict you be in ordinary, you have never, if this be your manner, come to a full determination; have never fully made choice of religion and the benefits of it for your only portion; and at best have got no further than king Agrippa, who was *almost* persuaded to be a Christian, Acts 26:28.--You are in the state of the stony-ground hearers, you have no root in yourselves, and like a tree without root, are easily blown down by every wind.

 II. I shall conclude with an earnest exhortation to all, no longer to halt between two opinions, but immediately to come to a determination whether to be Christians or not. Let me insist upon it, that you now make a choice, whether you will have heaven, with a life of universal and persevering obedience for your portion; or hell, with a life spent in the pursuit of this world.--Consider those things which have been said, shewing the unreasonableness of continuing in such irresolution about an affair of infinite importance to you, and to which you have so short an opportunity to make your choice. Consider two things in addition to what hath been already said.

 1. Those who live under the gospel, and thus continue undetermined about religion, are more abominable to God than the heathen. God had rather that men should either be Christians or downright heathens. He hates those persons who continue from year to year, under the calls, and warnings, and instructions, and intreaties of God's word; who yet can be brought to nothing; who will come to no determination at all; will neither be Christians nor heathens. These are they who are spoken of in Rev. 3:15-16. "I know thy works, that thou art neither cold nor hot: I would thou wert cold or hot. So then because thou are lukewarm, and neither cold nor hot, I will spew thee out of my mouth."--And Ezek. 20:39. "As for you, O house of Israel, thus saith the Lord God, Go ye, serve ye every one his idols, and hereafter also, if ye will not hearken unto me: but pollute ye my holy name no more with your gifts, and with your idols" These are they spoken of in 2 Tim. 3:7. "Ever learning and never coming to the knowledge of the truth."

 2. If you still refuse to come to a determination whether to be Christians or not, how just will it be, if God shall give you no further opportunity! If you refuse to make any choice at all; and after all that hath been done to bring you to it, in setting life and death so often before you; in calling and warning you, if you will not come to a determination, how just will it be, if God shall wait no longer upon you, if he shall, by

his unalterable sentence, determine the case himself; if he shall fix your state with the unbelievers, and teach you the truth and eligibleness of religion, by sad and fatal experience, when it will be too late for you to chuse your portion, and the offer will be no more made you!

Excerpted from
The Missionary Work; or, A Book for the Times
By W. Slaughter
Dayton, Ohio: The Trustees of the United Brethren Printing Establishment, 1856,
pp. 19-24

What tongue can describe, or pencil paint the miseries of the race to which we belong? So deeply steeped in vice and sensuality has it became, that as a legitimate result, its intellectual powers have dwindled down until they rise but little above the brute.

"The field is the world." Jesus Christ organized the church as a vast missionary society, and committed to its fostering care the interests of the whole world, as the field of its pious toils; and its work will not be completed until the *Watchmen* shall see, "eye to eye," and the echo of salvation shall have sounded upon the hill-tops, and in the valleys, until,

"From north to south the princes meet,
And pay their homage at his feet;
Whilst western empires own their Lord,
And savage tribes attend his word."

…. THE mission of the blessed Savior into this sin-cursed world, had for its object the dissemination of Evangelical Light and Truth, whereby the intellectual and moral darkness that shrouded the entire race in gloom, and bathed its brightest prospects in tears, might be rolled away. But for the effecting of this object,--one worthy of a God,--who supposes that he would have left the glory he had with the Father before the world was, and the smiles and adorations of admiring angels, for the dismal scenes of the garden of Gethsemane, Pilate's Bar, and the Cross of Calvary? Upon these grand subjects, into which angels desired to look, the great heart of the blessed Savior dwelt with such pleasurable emotions that the horrid scenes of Calvary seemed obscured in the attractions of the Cross. Imbued with this spirit to the fullest extent, wonder not at his beautiful exclamation, "I, if I be lifted up, will draw all men unto me."

    The term missionary means, one sent forth; hence, the blessed Savior informed the Jews that he was sent by the Father. "The title of Apostles, by which he saw it meet to designate his twelve chosen disciples, is but the rendering into Greek, as the learned inform us, the same idea which, borrowing the word from the language of the Romans, we express by the term missionary; and the Savior himself is by Paul described as the great Apostle of our Profession; or, in other words, the "chiefest Missionary of the Church." With great propriety may our blessed Lord be designated by this appellation, if we but transfer our minds to the source of this great Missionary, viz: the *Eternal Godhead*. This eminent Missionary voluntarily exiled himself from the society of angels, and the loveliness of the country that is afar off, and partook of our nature, became partner of our sorrows and eyewitness of our degradation and abominations. The field to which he came was emphatically a foreign one; far from his native home as the heavens are above the earth. The people to whom he came to minister in the character of an humble missionary, were miserably wasted, worn, depraved, and corrupted with crime. Though proscribed, persecuted, forsaken, maltreated, hunted as a partridge upon the mountains, forsaken of the Father, crowned with thorns, and nailed to the cross; yet, under all this he can pray, *"Father, forgive them,"* &c.

    The Savior of mankind lured no one to follow him, by the promise of ease, honors, wealth, or the laurels of this world; but plainly told the people that "the foxes have holes, the birds of the air have nests, but the Son of Man hath not where to lay his head." And again, that "the disciple is not above his Lord." As he missionated from place to place, he boldly attacked all the forms of popular and idolatrous worship, rooted up long established usages, upturned the tables of the money-changers, and insisted in their stead, on repentance toward God, and faith in our Lord Jesus Christ. This doctrine his forerunner published on the banks of the Jordan; *he himself*, wearied and faint, taught it at the well of Samaria, to a lone woman,--spoke it in the ear of his twelve chosen ones,--proclaimed it on the house-top,--illustrated it in parables, and demonstrated it by miracles.

Excerpted from
Sermons
by George Whitefield

Editor's note: My 18th Century copy is missing the title page, hence no place of publication, and no date. George Whitefield, 1714-1770, was an English clergyman who traveled and preached extensively throughout the American colonies. He influenced the "Great Awakening" and was a close friend of Benjamin Franklin who published several of his tracts.

… there is a time when the soul is benumbed, barren, and dry, and the believer has not a word to say to his heavenly Father; and then the heart only can speak. And I mention this for the encouragement of weak Christians, who think they never are accepted but when they have a flow of words, and fancy they do not please God at the bottom, for no other reason but because they do not please themselves. Such would do well to consider, that God knows the language of the heart, and the mind of the spirit; and that we make use of words, not to inform God, but to affect ourselves. Whenever therefore any of you find yourselves in such a frame, be not discouraged: offer yourselves up in silence before God, as clay in the hands of the potter, for him to write and stamp his own divine image upon your souls.

Excerpted from
Cardiphonia: of the Utterance of the Heart
By the Rev. John Newton
Edinburgh: Printed for Waugh and Innes, 1825, pp. 141-145.

Editor's note: John Henry Newton, 1725-1807, was a captain of slave-trading ships who repented, eventually became an evangelical lay-minister and later an Anglican priest and abolitionist. He is author of the Hymn "Amazing Grace."

The Christian is a new creature, born and taught from above. He has been convinced of his guilt and misery as a sinner, has fled for refuge to the hope set before him, has seen the Son and believed on him; his natural prejudices against the glory and grace of God's salvation have been subdued and silenced by almighty power; he has accepted the Beloved, and is made acceptable in him: he now knows the Lord; has renounced the confused, distant, uncomfortable notions he once formed of God; and beholds him in Christ, who is the way, the truth, and the life, the only door by which we can enter to any true satisfying knowledge of God, or communion with him. But he sees God in Christ reconciled, a Father, a Saviour, and a Friend, who has freely forgiven him all his sins, and given him the spirit of adoption: he is now no longer a servant, much less a stranger, but a son; and because a son, an heir already interested in all the promises, admitted to the throne of grace, and an assured expectant of eternal glory. The gospel is designed to give us not only a peradventure or a probability, but a certainty both of our acceptance and our perseverance, till death shall be swallowed up in life. And though many are sadly fluctuating and perplexed upon this head, and perhaps all are so for a season, yet there are those who can say, we know that we are of God; and therefore they are steadfast and unmovable in his way; because they are confident that their labour shall not be in vain, but that when they shall be absent from the body, they shall be present with the Lord. This is the state of the advanced experienced Christian, who being enabled to make his profession the chief business of his life, is strong in the Lord and in the power of his might. Every one who has this hope in Christ, purifieth himself even as he is pure. I would now attempt a sketch of the Christian's temper, formed upon these principles and hopes, under the leading branches of its exercise, respecting God, himself, and his fellow-creatures.

    The Christian's temper Godward is evidenced by *humility*. He has received from Gethsemane and Golgotha such a sense of the evil of sin, and of the holiness of God, combined with his matchless love to sinners, as has deeply penetrated his heart; he has an affecting remembrance of the state of rebellion and enmity in which he once lived against this holy and good God: and he has a quick perception of the defilements and defects which still debase his best services. His mouth is therefore stopped as to boasting; he is vile in his own eyes, and is filled with wonder that the Lord should visit such a sinner with such a salvation. He sees so vast a disproportion between the obligations he is under to grace, and the returns he makes, that he is disposed, yea, constrained, to adopt the apostle's words without affection, and to account himself less than the least of all saints; and knowing his own *heart* while he sees only the outside of others, he is not easily persuaded there can be a believer upon earth so faint, so unfruitful, so unworthy as himself. Yet, though abased, he is not discouraged, for he enjoys *peace*. The dignity, offices, blood, righteousness, faithfulness, and compassion of the Redeemer, in whom he rests, trusts, and lives, for wisdom, righteousness, sanctification, and redemption, are adequate to all his wants and wishes, provide him with an answer to every objection, and give him no less confidence in God, than if he were sinless as an angel: for he sees, that though sin has abounded in him, grace has much more abounded in Jesus. With respect to the past, all things are become new; with respect to the present and future, he leans upon an almighty arm, and relies upon the word and power which made and upholds the heavens and the earth. Though he feels himself unworthy of the smallest mercies, he claims and expects the greatest blessings that God can bestow; and being rooted and grounded in the knowledge and love of Christ, his peace abides, and is not greatly affected, either by the variation of his own frames, or the changes of God's dispensations towards him while here. With such a sense of himself, such a heart-felt peace and heavenly hope, how can his spirit but breathe *love* to his God and Saviour? It is indeed the perfection of his character and happiness, that his soul is united by love to the chief good. The love of Christ is the joy of his heart, and the spring of his obedience. With his Saviour's presence, he finds a heaven begun upon earth; and without it, all the other glories of the heavenly state would not content him. The excellence of Christ, his love to sinners, especially his dying love; his love to himself in seeking and saving him when lost, saving him to the uttermost--but I must stop.--

…(You) can better conceive than I can describe, how and why Jesus is dear to the heart that knows him. That part of the Christian's life which is not employed in the active service of his Lord, is chiefly spent in seeking and maintaining communion with him. For this he plies the throne, and studies the word of grace, and frequents the ordinances, where the Lord has promised to meet with his people. These are his golden hours; and when thus employed, how poor and trivial does all that the world calls great and important appear in his eyes! Yea, he is solicitous to keep up an intercourse of heart with his Beloved in his busiest scenes; and so far as he can succeed, it alleviates all his labours, and sweetens all his troubles. And when he is neither communing with his Lord, nor acting for him, he accounts his time lost, and is ashamed and grieved. The truth of his love is manifested by *submission*. This is twofold, and absolute and without reserve in each.--He submits to his revealed will, as made known to him by precept, and by his own example. He aims to tread in his Saviour's footsteps, and makes conscience of *all* his commandments, without exception and without hesitation. Again, he submits to his providential will: he yields to his sovereignty, acquiesces in his wisdom; he knows he has no *right* to complain of any thing, because he is a sinner; and he has no *reason*, because he is sure the Lord does all things well. Therefore his submission is not forced, but is in an act of *trust*. He knows he is not more unworthy than he is unable to choose for himself, and therefore rejoices that the Lord has undertaken to manage for him; and were he compelled to make his own choice, he could only choose, that all his concerns should remain in that hand to which he has already committed them. And thus he judges of *public* as well as of his personal affairs. He cannot be an unaffected spectator of national sins, nor without apprehension of their deserved consequences; he feels, and almost trembles for others; but he himself dwells under the shadow of the Almighty, in a sanctuary that cannot be forced; and therefore, should he see the earth shaken, and the mountains cast into the midst of the sea, his heart would not be greatly moved, for God is his refuge. The Lord reigns. He sees his Saviour's hands directing every dark appearance, and overruling all to the accomplishment of his own great purposes: this satisfies him; and though the winds and waves should be high, he can venture his own little bark in the storm, for he has an infallible and almighty pilot onboard with him. And indeed, why should he fear when he has nothing to love? His best concerns are safe; and other things he holds as gifts from his Lord, to whose call he is ready to resign them, in whatever way he pleases; well knowing, that creatures and instruments cannot of themselves touch a hair of his head without the Lord's permission, and that if he does permit them, it must be for the best.

Extracted from
A Practical View of Christian Education in its Early Stages
No author indicated
London: Printed for J. Hatchard and Son, by Ellerton and Henderson, 1820, 6th Edition, pp. 9-10 and 40-48

When parents, though they may have a great respect for religion, are not truly religious, there is no difficulty in accounting for their lukewarmness in providing for the religious education of their children. If they do not consider Christianity as the pearl of great price; if in practice they make it rather the handmaid of their worldly interests and pleasures, than the unrivalled empress of their hearts, and the sovereign guide of their actions: if this is *practically* the estimation in which they hold it, of course, they will give it but a second, a third, or a fourth place among the objects on which their view is fixed in the education of their children. If, in their passage through life, the do not *in fact* (whatever they may hold in theory) sacrifice their own profit, or pleasure, or reputation at the shrine of Religion, when these cannot be secured without some dereliction of duty, it must be expected that, whatever they may profess as to their plans of education, they will *in fact* attend more to the worldly advancement, or pleasure, or reputation of their children, than to their progress in vital Christianity. As such parents, however, frequently lament in themselves defects which they have not a heart to remedy; let them be asked whether they would willingly see their offspring in the same state…, pursuing a course which they disapprove, and breathing fruitless wishes after that holiness which they have not the courage to practice. If their minds revolt at this prospect, let them endeavour, in their choice of masters and instructors, to rescue their children at least from the evils which press upon themselves. They may think it impracticable in their own case (though in truth, if they undertook the work in a right spirit, they would conquer every difficulty by the all-powerful aid of Divine grace) ….

May parents, then, never relax with their children? Must they always sustain the grave character of a tutor? Most certainly they may, and ought, frequently to relax with them, and even to take pains to make them happy by joining in their little amusements: but they may combine this course of proceeding extremely well with a constant recollection of the immortal nature and high value of their children, for whom Christ died, and with a suitable behaviour towards them. A father will soon learn, in such playful moments, "miscere utile dulci;" or, according to our English proverb, to "be merry and wise;" and he will rank such seasons among those which are most important for checking what is wrong in a child, fostering what is right, instilling good principles, infusing a just appreciation of things, and a taste for what is lovely and of good report. All the good seed sown on such occasions will be so combined with the child's pleasures and affections, as, with God's blessing, to take deep root in the soul, and promise a vigorous and permanent growth.

In managing a child, let a parent always have the child's good, rather than his own ease, In view....

In correcting a fault, look to the heart rather than to the outward act.

How common it is for parents to pursue the opposite course! They are satisfied with condemning and preventing wrong conduct, without much attending to the temper of mind in which their animadversions are received; and the child is often left unhumbled and discontented, and in a state as displeasing to God as when it was committing the fault in question. This mode of proceeding appears to me essentially wrong, and productive of serious evil. It does not bring the child to repentance before God, and to peace with him. It directs its view to the maintenance of decency in externals, rather than to a jealous scrutiny of its motives and dispositions, and an earnest desire of reconciliation with its God, after having offended him. Though these marks of true repentance cannot be expected at so early an age in their full extent, yet a broad foundation for them is often laid during the two or three first years of infancy. On the other hand, when we see a child scowl, or snatch up his shoulders, or pout and redden, on being blamed, can the r rebellious and unbending spirit within him be doubted? Is he humbled for his fault, and in a spirit to forsake it and seek forgiveness?

Is there any putting off of the old man, and putting on of the new man? And yet, can it be denied, that this is the only temper to which the promise of pardon is made? It is the temper in which adults must come to Christ for pardon and peace; and it is therefore the temper to which, from the very dawn of reason, we should endeavour to bring children.

In our endeavours to effect this great object, kind and mild and serene, but unyielding, perseverance is to be employed. There must be neither violence nor hurry., If the child is impatient, some constraint, if necessary, must be used to prevent ebullitions of passion or fretfulness, and time must be given for it to recover itself; then steady and unwearied, but calm and affectionate, addresses to its reason and feelings, suited to its age, and habits, and natural disposition, must be employed. The sagacity and ingenuity of the parent must be tasked to select the best topics, and handle them in the best manner for the production of the desired effect. But, above all, his eye must be upon God for guidance and a blessing, and for putting his own mind in the frame best adapted to win upon the affections of the child, and impress his heart. The dawnings of a right spirit in him must be hailed; openness and confidence must be courted and encouraged; the kindness of God and Christ to penitents must be fully and touchingly portrayed as their hatred of sin. Care must be taken not to overstrain or overpower the feelings; and when any danger of doing so appears, a pause must take place till they are relieved, and self-command is regained. This course admits of great variations, and must be carefully adapted to the age and character and attainments of the child: but I think I can say from experience, that it will seldom if ever fail of ultimate success, if steadily and habitually pursued. It may be said to begin from nothing; and for several months a very small part of it will be brought forwards, though there will be a continual progress as the mind of the child opens, and *something* right in moral feeling and habit is established. He will begin to learn the difference between being good and naughty; then, that though he desists from doing a naughty thing, he continues naughty till he is sorry for it and good humoured; and then, and not till then, he may expect the kiss of forgiveness, and regain the favour of his parent. Next he will be taught to reflect on his happiness when good, and on the pain he suffers when naughty; and he will be told that this is from God, who loves goodness and hates naughtiness, as he sees his parents do. Then he will proceed to learn that, like his parents, God expects sorrow for sin, and a mild and humbler prayer for forgiveness, before he will forgive a naughty child, and love him, and make him happy. While this is in progress, the parent will endeavour to make the child feel the evil and folly of naughtiness, and the beauty and true wisdom of being good. This will not be very difficult to inculcate, when the child is sensible that sin and misery, and holiness and happiness, generally go together. During the latter part of this course, gospel facts and principles will be gradually opened. The child will have heard of Christ ever since he first heard of God; and now the distinct character and offices of Christ will begin to be unfolded. He will be painted as the Friend of mankind; as the great Refuge of all who have done wrong; as always willing to help them, and beg his Father to forgive them;--as all kindness and goodness, and as setting us an example of all that is lovely and excellent; and as now exalted in glory, and all-wise, and all-powerful. Pains will be taken to make him the object of affection at tempered by reverence, and to make it pleasant to the child to please him, and painful to offend him. The child will in like manner be made acquainted with the Holy Ghost, and heaven, and hell, and the day of judgment, and eternity, and the lost state of man, and redemption. All these things will be taught with an immediate reference to practice and the heart. They must be unfolded gradually, and with a strict attention to the abilities and temperament of the child; and especial care must be taken, that by God's blessing the feelings shall be properly affected as the understanding is informed.

Extracted from
The Wonderful Works of God Are to Be Remembered--
A Sermon Delivered on the Day of Annual Thanksgiving, November 20, 1794

By David Osgood, Pastor of the Church in Medford
Boston: Printed by Samuel Hall, 1794, Second Edition, pp. 9-12

At certain periods of time, through the several ages and among the different nations of the world, God breaks forth in signal and remarkable dispensations for the relief of the righteous, or for the punishment of the wicked. His providence is seen justifying its own procedure in vindicating and delivering oppressed innocence, or in precipitating prosperous guilt from its lofty seat. On these occasions, God is known by the glory that surrounds him. Beholding these extraordinary proofs of his presence and power, men are constrained to say, *Verily there is a reward for the righteous: verily he is a God that judgeth in the earth.*

And when we are once established in the belief of such a great and glorious Being, this faith will naturally prompt us to fear and serve him. Convinced of his power and justice by the awful manifestations of them in his works, we shall be led to stand in awe of him, and heedfully to shun whatever we apprehend to be offensive in his sight. Struck with the more signal displays of his mercy and goodness, and excited by them to the more fixed contemplation of his unbounded beneficence; we shall be satisfied, that our happiness must consist in the enjoyment of his favour. This persuasion will render us anxious to know *what the Lord our God requires of us*; and solicitous to approve ourselves to him, by a patient continuance in well-doing.

Our present trust in the divine mercy is also encouraged by the remembrance of former favours and deliverances. For this purpose, among others, the Israelites were enjoined to teach "their children the praises of the Lord, his strength, and his wonderful works--that the generation to come might know them--even the children which should be born: who should arise and declare them to their children; that they might set their HOPE in God."

The honour of God, the interests of religion, and the comfort and consolation of good men, being all promoted by the memory of the divine dispensations; it is highly agreeable to reason, and consonant to scripture, that public days should be set apart, on which a whole people may unite in celebrating the goodness of Gold; recollecting the instances of his providential care of, and kindness towards, them; and talking of his wonderful works in their favour. Such institutions serve as *pillars of remembrance,* to revive and perpetuate a sense of our obligations to Heaven. The thoughts of the great body of the people are so taken up about their own private affairs, that they are prone to pay but little attention to the concerns of the public. After the first impression is worn off, they soon forget, at least practically, national mercies and deliverances, as well as national judgments. They need to have their minds stirred up by way of remembrance. And when God, by a long and continued series of remarkable interpositions, has multiplied, blessed, and prospered any people--has, on one occasion and another, repeatedly rescued them from great and threatening dangers--put them in full possession of their rights and liberties, laws and religion; and from year to year continues them in the quiet enjoyment of these privileges, together with the usual bounties of his munificent providence; they cannot too frequently recollect, nor too fervently and gratefully acknowledge, these signal instances of the divine benignity. It surely becomes christian magistrates, and is a duty they owe to God, to call upon their subjects to unite in commemorating these wonderful words of Heaven in their favour.

    Our forefathers, from the first settlement of the country, esteemed certain seasons of the year as highly proper for special acts of devotion. At the opening of the spring, they judged it fit and suitable, to set apart a day for humiliation and prayer; that they might implore the divine blessing on the affairs of the ensuing season--that it might be rendered fruitful, healthy and prosperous. And after the reception of these mercies, at the close of the season, another day was set apart for public thanksgiving. To this custom of our *pious and renowned ancestors* the proclamation for the observance of this day expressly refers. To the friends of religion among us it must be highly agreeable, to join in making this day a grateful memorial of God's providential kindness towards us; and especially, in recording the more signal mercies of the last revolving season….

    On this day it becomes us, with increased love and thankfulness to pay our vows to that Being who is the health of our countenance and the God of our lives….

Excerpted from
Sermons on the Security and Happiness of a Virtuous Course...

by Richard Price, Fellow of the American Philosophical Societies at Philadelphia and Boston
Boston: Printed by E. W. Weld and W. Greenough for John West, 1794, pp. 36-41

I have already observed, that virtue leaves us in possession of all the common enjoyments of life. It is necessary now to add, that it goes much beyond this. --It not only leaves us in possession of all innocent and natural pleasures; but improves and refines them. It not only interferes *less* with the gratification of our different powers than vice does; but renders the gratification of many of them *more* the cause of pleasure. This effect it produces by restraining us to regularity and moderation in the gratification of our desires. Virtue forbids only the wild and extravagant gratification of our desires: That is, it forbids only such a gratification of them as goes beyond the bounds of nature, and lays the foundation of pain and misery. As far as they were designed by our Maker to yield pleasure, we are at liberty to indulge them; and farther we cannot go without losing pleasure. --It is a truth generally acknowledged, that the regular and moderate gratification of appetite is more agreeable than any forced and exorbitant gratification of it. Excess in every way is painful and pernicious. We can never contradict nature without suffering, and bringing upon ourselves inconveniences. --It there any man to whom food and sleep are so pleasant as to the temperate man? Are the mad and polluted joys of the fornicator and adulterer equal to the pure and chaste joys of the married state? Do pampered and loaded appetites afford as much delight as appetites kept under discipline, and never palled by riot and licentiousness? Is the vile glutton, the loathsome drunkard, or the rotten debauchee, as happy as the sober and virtuous man who has a healthful body, a serene mind, and general credit?

  Thus is virtue a friend even to appetite. But this is not the observation I intended to insist on. What I meant here principally to recommend to your attention was, that virtue improves all the blessings of life, by putting us into a particular disposition for receiving pleasure from them. It removes those internal evils which pollute and impair the springs of enjoyment within us. It renders the mind easy and satisfied within itself, and therefore more susceptible of delight, and more open to all agreeable impressions. It is a common observation, that the degree of pleasure which we receive from any objects depends on the disposition we are in to receive pleasure. Nothing is sweet to a depraved taste; nothing beautiful to a distempered eye. This observation holds with particular force in the present case. Vice destroys the relish of sensible pleasures. It takes off (I may say) from the fruit its flavour, and from the rose its hue. It tarnishes the beauty of nature, and communicates a bitter tincture to every enjoyment. --Virtue, on the contrary, sweetens every blessing, and throws new luster on the face of nature. It chases away gloominess and peevishness; and, by strengthening the kind affections, and introducing into the soul good-humour and tranquility, makes every pleasing scene and occurrence more pleasing.

… Let us consider how many *peculiar* joys virtue has which nothing else can give. It is not possible to enumerate all these. We may, on this occasion, recollect first those joys which necessarily spring from the worthy and generous affections. The love of the Deity, benevolence, meekness, and gratitude, are by their nature attended with pleasure. They put the mind into a serene and cheerful frame, and introduce into it some of the most delightful sensations. Virtue consists in the exercise and cultivation of these principles. They form the temper, and constitute the character of a virtuous man; and, therefore, he must enjoy pleasure to which men of a contrary character are strangers. --It is not conceivable, that a person in whom the mild and generous affections thrive, should not be in a more happy state than one who counteracts and suppresses them; and who, instead of feeling the joy which springs up in a heart where the heavenly graces and virtues reside, is torn and distracted by anger, malice, and envy.

But further; Peace of conscience is another blessing peculiar to virtue. It reconciles us to ourselves as well as to all the world. As nothing can be so horrid as to be at variance with one's self, so nothing can be so delightful as to be at peace with one's self. If we are unhappy within our own breasts, it signifies little what external advantages we enjoy. If we want *our own* approbation, it is of little consequence how much *others* applaud us. Virtue secures to us our own approbation. It reduces to harmony, under the dominion of conscience all our jarring powers. It makes our reflections agreeable to us; and the mind a fund of comfort to itself.

Again; A sense of God's favour is another source of pleasure which is peculiar to virtue. The Divine government is an object of terror to a wicked man. He cannot think of it without trouble. But a virtuous man derives his chief consolations from hence. He is conscious of acting in concert with the Deity, of obeying his laws, and of imitating his perfections. He, therefore, exults in the assurance of having him on his side, and of being under his Almighty protection. He knows that the Sovereign of the universe loves him, and is his unalterable friend.

Once more. A virtuous man possesses the hope of a future reward. Every one knows how mighty the power of hope is to invigorate and cheer the mind. There is no such hope as that of the virtuous man. He hopes for a perfect government in the heavens; and this comforts him amidst all the disorders of earthly governments. He hopes for a resurrection from death to a blessed immortality. He expects soon to take possession of a treasure in the heavens that faileth not; to receive an incorruptible inheritance; to exchange ignorance and doubt for knowledge; and to be fixed in that world where he shall join superior beings, and be always growing more wise, and good, and great, and happy, till some time or other he shall rise to honours and powers which are no more possible to be now conceived by him, than the powers of an angel can be conceived by a child in the womb. --This is indeed an unbounded and ravishing hope. If Christianity is true, we have abundant reason for it. Christ came into the world to raise us to it; and the most distant glimmering of it, is enough to eclipse all the glory of this world.

Such are the singular blessings of the virtuous man.

Excerpted from The Second Part of Logick.

Chap. III "The Springs of false Judgment, or the Doctrine of Prejudices" in

Logick: or, the Right Use of Reason in the Enquiry after Truth

by Isaac Watts, D. D.
London: (no publisher/printer indicated), 1754, the Tenth Edition.

Editor's note: In today's America we are fond of demonizing persons holding viewpoints differing from our own, especially in the area of politics. The following discourse identifies the error of associating a particular political position with Christianity. Just because one seeks to make one's own viewpoint the "Christian viewpoint" and those viewpoints which differ as "unchristian" doesn't necessarily make it so. Our nation is now being stressed and weakened by those who sow discord. Civility, respect for others, cooperation, and, common sense need to reaffirmed and defended if we are to remain a strong, free, and providence-protected people. Such values are indeed a part of our American Christian Heritage.

…. What remains in this *Second Part of Logick* is to point out the several *Springs and Causes of our Mistakes* in judging, and to lay down some *Rules* by which we should conduct ourselves in passing a Judgment of every thing that is proposed to us….

Rash judgments are called *prejudices*, and so are the springs of them…. Sometimes these rash judgments are called *prepossessions,* whereby is meant, that some particular opinion has possessed the mind, and engaged the assent the assent without sufficient search or evidence of the truth of it.

There is a vast variety of these prejudices and prepossessions which attend mankind in every age and condition of life; they lay the foundations of many an error, and many an unhappy practice, both in the affairs of religion, and in our civil concernments; as well as in matters of learning. It is necessary for a man who pursues truth to enquire into these *springs of error*, that as far as possible he may rid himself of old prejudices, and watch hourly against new ones....

The first sort of prejudices are those which arise from the things themselves about which we judge....

I. *The obscurity of some truths, and the difficulty of searching them out*, is one occasion of rash and mistaken judgment.... In many of these cases, a great part of mankind is not content to be entirely ignorant; but they rather chuse to form rash and hasty judgment, to guess at things without just evidence, to believe something concerning them before they can know them, and thereby they fall into error.

This sort of prejudice, as well as most others, is cured by patience and diligence in enquiry and reasoning, and a suspension of judgment, till we have attained some proper mediums of knowledge, and till we see sufficient evidence of the truth.

II. *The appearance of things in a disguise*, is another spring of prejudice or rash judgment. The outside of things which first strikes us, is oftentimes different from their inward nature, and we are tempted to judge suddenly according to outward appearances…. So the scholar spies the name of a new book in publick newspapers, he is charmed with the title, he purchases, he reads with huge expectations, and finds it all trash and impertinence; this is a prejudice derived from the *appearance*; we are too ready to judge the volume valuable which had so good a frontispiece….

III. *A mixture of different qualities in the same thing*, is another temptation to judge amiss. We are ready to be carried away by that quality which strikes the first or the strongest impressions upon us, and we judge of the whole object according to that quality, regardless of all the rest; or sometimes we colour over all the other qualities with that one tincture, whether it be bad or good….

This sort of prejudice is relieved by learning to distinguish things well, and not to judge in the lump. There is scarce any thing in the world of nature or art, in the world of morality or religion, that is perfectly uniform. There is a mixture of wisdom and folly, vice and virtue, good and evil, both in men and things…. We should neither praise nor dispraise by wholesale, but separate the good from the evil, and judge of them apart. The accuracy of a good judgment consists much in making such distinctions….

IV. Though a thing be uniform in its own nature, yet the *different lights in which it may be placed, and the different views in which it appears to us*, will be ready to excite in us mistaken judgments concerning it. Let an erect cone be placed in a horizontal plane, at a great distance from the eye, and it appears a plain triangle; but we shall judge that very cone to be nothing but a flat circle, if its base be obverted towards us.... The true method of delivering ourselves from this prejudice is to view a thing on all sides, to compare all the various appearances of the same thing with one another, and let each of them have its full weight in the balance of our judgment, before we fully determine our opinion....

    V. The *causal association of many of our ideas* becomes the spring of another prejudice or rash judgment, to which we are sometimes exposed.... It is for (this)... reason that the bulk of the common people are so superstitiously fond of the Psalms translated by Hopkins and Sternhold, and think them sacred and divine, because they have been now for more than an hundred years bound up in the same covers with our Bibles.

    The best relief against this prejudice of association, is to consider, whether there be any natural and necessary connexion between those ideas which fancy, custom, or chance hath thus joined together: And if nature has not joined them, let our judgment correct the follow of our imagination, and separate those ideas again.

Excerpted from
An Earnest Appeal to Men of Reason and Religion
by John Wesley
Dublin: Printed by John Jones for the Methodist Book-Room, 1806, pp. 22-25.

Editor's note: John Wesley, 1703-1791, was an Anglican cleric who, with his brother Charles, is largely credited with founding the "Methodist" movement.

Do you say in your heart, "I know all this already. I am not barely a man of reason. I am a religious man; for I not only avoid evil and do good, but use all the means of grace. I am constantly at church, and at the sacrament too. I say my prayers every day. I read many good books. I fast--every *Thirtieth of January, and Good-Friday.*" Do you indeed? Do you do all this! This you may do! You may go thus far, and yet have *no religion* at all; *no such religion* avails before God. Nay, much farther than this, than you have ever gone yet, or so much as thought of going. For you may *give all your goods to feed the poor,* yea, *your body to be burned,* and yet very possibly, if St. Paul be a judge, *have no charity,* no true religion.

This religion, which alone is of value before God, is the very thing you want. You want (and in wanting this, you want all) the religion of love. You do not love your neighbour as yourself, no more than you love God with all your heart. Ask your own heart now, if it be not so? It is plain you do not love God. If you did you would be happy in him. But you know you are not happy. Your *formal* religion no more makes you happy, than your neighbour's gay religion does him. O how much have you suffered for want of plain dealing! Can you now bear to hear the naked truth? You have *the form of godliness*, but not *the power*. You are a mere whited wall. Before the Lord your God I ask you, Are you not? Too sure. For your *inward parts are very wickedness*. You love the *creature more than the Creator*. You are *a lover of pleasure more than a lover of God*. A lover of God! You do not love God at all, no more than you love a stone. You love the world; therefore the love of the Father is not in you.

    You are on the brink of the pit, ready to be plunged into everlasting perdition. Indeed you have a zeal for God: but not according to knowledge. O how terribly have you been deceived! Posting to hell, and fancying it was heaven. See, at length that *outward religion* without *inward*, is nothing; is far worse than nothing, being indeed no other than a solemn mockery of God. And *inward religion you have not*. You have not the faith *that worketh by love*. Your *faith* (so called) is no living saving principle. It is not the Apostle's Faith, *the substance* (or subsistence) *of things hoped for, the evidence of things not seen*. So far from it, that this Faith is the very thing which you call *enthusiasm*. You are not content with being without it, unless you blaspheme it too. You even revile that *lie which is hid with* Christ *in* God. These things are *foolishness unto* you. No marvel; *or they are spiritually discerned.*

Oh! No longer shut your eyes against the light. Know you have a name that you live, but are dead. Your soul is utterly dead in sin; dead in pride, in vanity, in self-will, in sensuality, in love of the world. You are utterly dead to God. There is no intercourse between your soul and God. *You have neither seen him*, (by faith, as our Lord witnessed against them of old time) *nor heard his voice at any time*. You have no spiritual *senses exercised to discern spiritual good and evil*. You are angry at infidels, and are all the while as mere an infidel before God as they. You have *eyes that see not, and ears that hear not*. You have a *callous, unfeeling* heart.

Bear with me a little longer: my soul is distressed for you. *The good of this world hath blinded your eyes,* and you are *seeking death in the error of your life*. Because you do not commit gross sin, because you give alms, and go to church and sacrament, you imagine that you are serving God; yet in very deed you are serving the devil. For you are doing still your own will, not the will of God your Saviour. You are pleasing yourself in all you do. Pride, vanity, and self-will, (the genuine fruits of an earthly, sensual, devilish heart) pollute all your words and actions. You are in darkness, in the shadow of death. Oh! that God would say to you in thunder, *Awake thou that sleepeth, and arise from the dead, and Christ shall give thee light.*

But blessed be God! He hath not yet left himself without witness!

"The Meditation of a Sinner, who was once thoughtless,
but begins to be awakened."
Excerpted from
The Rise and Progress of Religion in the Soul
by Philip Doddridge
Brattleborough: John Holbrook, 1816

Editor's note: Philip Doddridge, 1702-1751, was an English "Nonconformist" leader and educator. Reading this book, The Rise and Progress of Religion in the Soul, led William Wilberforce to become a Christian. Wilberforce was a British politician who campaigned for the abolition of slavery. His efforts were largely responsible for the passage of the Slave Abolition Act of 1833 which abolished slavery in most of the British Empire. Charles Spurgeon referred to The Rise and Progress of Religion in the Soul, as "that holy book".

AWAKE, oh my forgetful soul, awake from these wandering dreams; turn thee from this chase of vanity, and for a little while be persuaded, by all these considerations, to look forward, and to look upwards, at least for a few moments. Sufficient are the hours and days given to the labors and amusements of life; grudge not a short allotment of minutes to view thyself and thine own more immediate concerns; to reflect who, and what thou art; how it comes to pass that thou art here, and what thou must quickly be!

It is indeed as thou hast now seen it represented. Oh my soul, thou are the creature of

God, formed and furnished by him, and lodged in a body in which he intended thee only a transitory abode. O think how soon *this tabernacle must be dissolved*, and thou must *return to God.* And shall He the one infinite eternal, ever blessed, and ever glorious Being, shall He be least of all regarded by thee? Wilt thou live and die with this character, saying by every action of every day unto God, *Depart from me for I desire not the knowledge of thy ways*? The morning, the day, the evening, the night, every period of time, has its excuses for this neglect. But, oh my soul, what will these excuses appear when examined by his penetrating eye! They may delude me, but they cannot impose upon him.

Oh thou injured, neglected, provoked Benefactor! when I think but for a moment or two, of all they goodness, I am astonished at this insensibility which hath prevailed in my heart, and even still prevails. *I blush and am confounded to lift up my face before thee.* On the most transient review, I see that *I have played the fool, that I have erred exceedingly*; and yet this stupid heart of mine would make its having neglected thee so long, a reason for going on to neglect thee. I own it might justly be expected that, with regard to thee, every one of thy rational creatures should be all duty and love; that each heart should be full of a sense of thy presence; and that a care to please thee should swallow up every other care; yet thou *hast not been in all my thoughts*; and religion, the end and glory of my nature, has been so strangely overlooked, that I have hardly ever seriously asked my own heart what it is. I know if matters rest here, I perish; and yet I feel in my perverse nature a secret indisposition to pursue these thoughts; a proneness, if not entirely to dismiss them, yet to lay them aside for the present. My mind is perplexed and divided; but I am sure thou who madest me knowest what is best for me. I, therefore, beech thee, that thou wilt, *for thy name's sake lead me and guide me.* Let me not delay till it is forever too late; *pluck me as a brand out of the burning.* Oh, break this fatal enchantment that holds down my affections to objects which my judgment comparatively despises! and let me at length, come into so happy a state of mind, that I may not be afraid to think of thee and of myself; and may not be tempted to wish, that thou hadst not made me; or that thou couldst forever forget me: That it may not be my best hope to perish like the brutes.

If what I shall farther read here be agreeable to truth and reason; if it be calculated to promote my happiness, and is to be regarded as an intimation of thy will and pleasure to me, of God, let me hear and obey; let the words of thy servant, when pleading thy cause be like goads to pierce into my mind; and let me rather feel, and smart, than die! let them be as *nails fastened in a sure place*: That whatever mysteries yet unknown, or whatever difficulties there be in religion, if it be necessary, I may not finally neglect it; and that if it be expedient to attend immediately to it, I may no longer delay that attendance! And, oh! let thy grace teach me the lesson I am so slow to learn, and conquer that strong opposition which I feel in my heart against the very thought of it! Hear these broken cries for the sake of thy Son, who has taught and saved many a creature as untractable as I, and can *out of stones raise up children to Abraham. Amen.*

www.ingramcontent.com/pod-product-compliance
Lightning Source LLC
Chambersburg PA
CBHW061640040426
42446CB00010B/1503